Spaghetti Alla Norma, page 16

Cooking Light.
Italian

Oxmoor House.

©2006 by Oxmoor House, Inc.
Book Division of Southern Progress Corporation
P.O. Box 2262, Birmingham, Alabama 35201

ISBN-13: 978-0-8487-3067-3
ISBN-10: 0-8487-3067-4
Library of Congress Control Number:
2006929982
Printed in the United States of America
First printing 2006

Be sure to check with your health-care provider
before making any changes in your diet.

Oxmoor House, Inc.
Editor in Chief: Nancy Fitzpatrick Wyatt
Executive Editor: Katherine M. Eakin
Copy Chief: Allison Long Lowery

Cooking Light® Italian
Editor: Heather Averett
Copy Editor: Jacqueline Giovanelli
Editorial Assistant: Julie Boston
Nutrition Editorial Assistant:
    Rachel Quinlivan, R.D.
Photography Director: Jim Bathie
Senior Photo Stylist: Kay E. Clarke
Photo Stylist: Katherine Eckert
Director, Test Kitchens: Elizabeth Tyler Austin
Assistant Director, Test Kitchens:
    Julie Christopher
Test Kitchens Staff: Nicole Lee Faber,
    Kathleen Royal Phillips
Food Stylist: Kelley Self Wilton
Director of Production: Laura Lockhart
Senior Production Manager: Greg A. Amason
Production Manager: Tamara Nall
Production Assistant: Faye Porter Bonner

Contributors:
Designer: Carol Damsky
Indexer: Mary Ann Laurens
Editorial Interns: Jill Baughman, Ashley Leath,
    Caroline Markunas, Mary Katherine Pappas,
    Vanessa Rusch Thomas, Lucas Whittington
Photographers: Beau Gustafson, Lee Harrelson
Photo Stylist: Lydia DeGaris-Pursell

To order additional publications, call
1-800-765-6400, or visit oxmoorhouse.com

CONTENTS

Essential Italian   8

Enjoy the classics of Italian cuisine:
crunchy, tomato-topped bruschetta;
colorful, cheesy pizza; and al dente
spaghetti with sauce. You'll find these
and other favorite Italian recipes that no
Cooking Light cook should be without.

Antipasti, Soup & Salad   34

From a sweet-salty starter of melon
and prosciutto to a hearty, bean-and-
veggie–laden minestrone to a crisp,
garden-fresh Caesar salad, these recipes
showcase the Italian way of cooking—
always fresh and always simple.

Pasta, Risotto & Polenta   58

Steaming bowls and plates of tender
pasta, creamy risotto, and warm, thick
polenta evoke comfort like few other
foods.

Entrées 80

Fresh-from-the-sea shrimp scampi, fall-off-the bone tender lamb shanks, and juicy mustard-crusted beef tenderloin are among our best kitchen-tested Italian main dishes.

Bread, Panini & Pizza 102

A truly authentic Italian meal is served with *pane*, whether it's a ciabatta loaf, a focaccia panini, or the crisp crust of a wood-oven baked pizza.

Desserts 116

Italian desserts can be as straightforward as mixed marinated fruit or silky, panna cotta. Or they can be as splendid as sweet honey gelato or a slice of rich, tender, chocolaty cake.

Cooking Class   134
Subject Index   142
Recipe Index   143

Cooking Light®
Editor in Chief: Mary Kay Culpepper
Executive Editor: Billy R. Sims
Art Director: Susan Waldrip Dendy
Managing Editor: Maelynn Cheung
Senior Food Editor: Alison Mann Ashton
Features Editor: Phillip Rhodes
Projects Editor: Mary Simpson Creel, M.S., R.D.
Food Editor: Ann Taylor Pittman
Associate Food Editors: Julianna Grimes Bottcher,
    Timothy Q. Cebula
Assistant Food Editor: Kathy C. Kitchens, R.D.
Assistant Editors: Cindy Hatcher,
    Brandy Rushing
Test Kitchens Director: Vanessa Taylor Johnson
Senior Food Stylist: Kellie Gerber Kelley
Food Stylist: M. Kathleen Kanen
Test Kitchens Professionals: Sam Brannock,
    Kathryn Conrad, Mary H. Drennen,
    Jan Jacks Moon, Tiffany Vickers,
    Mike Wilson
Assistant Art Director: Maya Metz Logue
Senior Designers: Fernande Bondarenko,
    J. Shay McNamee
Designer: Brigette Mayer
Senior Photographer: Randy Mayor
Senior Photo Stylist: Cindy Barr
Photo Stylists: Melanie J. Clarke, Jan Gautro
Studio Assistant: Celine Chenoweth
Copy Chief: Maria Parker Hopkins
Senior Copy Editor: Susan Roberts
Copy Editor: Johannah Paiva
Production Manager: Liz Rhoades
Production Editors: Joanne McCrary Brasseal,
    Hazel R. Eddins
Administrative Coordinator: Carol D. Johnson
Office Manager: Rita K. Jackson
Editorial Assistant: Melissa Hoover
Correspondence Editor: Michelle Gibson Daniels
Interns: Sabrina Bone, Kimberly Burnstad,
    Melissa Marek, Molly Kate Matthews,
    Megan Voelkel

CookingLight.com
Editor: Jennifer Middleton Richards
Online Producer: Abigail Masters

Cover: *Herbed Chicken Parmesan* (page 98)

Welcome

Italian cuisine is versatile, sensual, and utterly enjoyable. But there's also another thing that Italian cuisine is, and that's essential. For a *Cooking Light*® cook, Italian-inspired dishes embody a cuisine that embraces fresh flavors and healthfulness in equal measure.

In this cookbook, you'll find the Italian recipes we believe to be essential for every *Cooking Light* cook. These recipes are our fresh interpretations of tried-and-true classics—ones we love to make again and again.

Each chapter offers mouthwatering, flavorful recipes, complete with nutritional analyses that will help you eat smart, be fit, and live well.

So whether you're looking for an easy appetizer like Tomato Crostini or for something a little more substantial, such as Veal Marsala, you're sure to find it in this edition of *The Cooking Light Cook's Essential Recipe Collection*.

Very truly yours,

Mary Kay Culpepper
Editor in Chief

essential italian

Tomato Bruschetta

There's no need to chop or slice the tomato for this easy dish. Instead, choose tomatoes that are firm, but juicy. Slice them in half and rub across the bread. The rough texture of the bread works like a grater to shred the flesh, and the tomato skin keeps the process from being too mushy.

8 (2-ounce) slices Italian or sourdough bread
4 garlic cloves, halved
4 small tomatoes, each cut in half crosswise (about ¾ pound)
4 teaspoons extravirgin olive oil
¼ teaspoon kosher salt or sea salt
¼ teaspoon freshly ground black pepper

1. Prepare grill.
2. Place bread slices on grill rack; grill 2 minutes on each side or until lightly browned. Rub 1 side of each bread slice with 1 garlic clove half and 1 tomato half (tomato pulp will rub off onto bread). Discard tomato peels. Drizzle ½ teaspoon olive oil over each bread slice; sprinkle evenly with salt and pepper. Yield: 8 servings (serving size: 1 slice).

CALORIES 168 (19% from fat); FAT 3.5g (sat 0.6g, mono 2.1g, poly 0.5g); PROTEIN 5.5g; CARB 29.3g; FIBER 1.4g; CHOL 0mg; IRON 1.6mg; SODIUM 351mg; CALC 60mg

Bruschetta is a derivative of the Italian verb bruscare, *which translates "to roast over coals." Originating in Tuscany, traditional bruschetta (broo-SKEH-tah) is toasted bread that's rubbed with garlic cloves, drizzled with olive oil, and sprinkled with coarse salt. Tomatoes were first discovered in the New World and imported into Italy in the 16th century. They didn't become a major ingredient in Italian cuisine until the 18th century. Rubbing the bread with tomato is a relatively new addition to this traditional recipe.*

Pasta e Fagioli

Fagioli (fa-ZHOH-lee) is Italian for "beans," and the type of bean used in recipes varies from region to region. Cannellini beans, also called white kidney beans, are commonly used in Pasta e Fagioli. Canned cannellini beans are a good choice for this soup since they're convenient and hold their shape during the short cook time.

1 tablespoon olive oil
6 ounces hot turkey Italian sausage
1½ tablespoons bottled minced garlic
1 cup water
1 (14-ounce) can fat-free, less-sodium chicken broth
1 (8-ounce) can no salt–added tomato sauce
1 cup uncooked small seashell pasta (about 4 ounces)
½ cup (2 ounces) shredded Romano cheese, divided
1½ teaspoons dried oregano
¼ teaspoon salt
¼ teaspoon white pepper
2 (15.5-ounce) cans cannellini beans or other white beans, drained
Minced fresh parsley (optional)

1. Heat oil in a large saucepan over medium-high heat. Add sausage and garlic; sauté 2 minutes or until browned, stirring to crumble. Add water, broth, and tomato sauce; bring to a boil. Stir in pasta, ¼ cup cheese, oregano, salt, white pepper, and beans; bring to a boil. Cover, reduce heat, and simmer 8 minutes or until pasta is done. Let stand 5 minutes; sprinkle each serving with cheese. Garnish with parsley, if desired. Yield: 6 servings (serving size: 1 cup soup and 2 teaspoons cheese).

CALORIES 244 (29% from fat); FAT 7.9g (sat 2.7g, mono 3g, poly 1.2g); PROTEIN 13g; CARB 27.7g; FIBER 4.4g; CHOL 24mg; IRON 4.9mg; SODIUM 836mg; CALC 129mg

Take a lesson in quick cooking from Italians with this hearty, comforting soup that's ready in less than 30 minutes. Hot turkey sausage, mellow cannellini beans, and tender seashell pasta combine to create a speedy weeknight dinner.

Insalata Caprese

2 large red tomatoes, each cut
  into 4 slices
2 large yellow tomatoes, each
  cut into 4 slices
6 (1-ounce) slices part-skim
  mozzarella cheese, each cut
  in half
12 large basil leaves
3 tablespoons fat-free
  balsamic vinaigrette
1 teaspoon freshly ground
  black pepper

1. Stack 4 tomato slices, 3 cheese slices, and 3 basil leaves in each of 4 stacks, alternating tomato, cheese, and basil. Drizzle stacks evenly with vinaigrette. Cover and chill. Sprinkle with pepper before serving. Yield: 4 servings.

CALORIES 172 (47% from fat); FAT 9g (sat 5.5g, mono 2.5g, poly 0.5g); PROTEIN 13g; CARB 11g; FIBER 2g; CHOL 23mg; IRON 1mg; SODIUM 404mg; CALC 336mg

Whether nestled between ripe tomatoes or melted over a bed of pasta, mozzarella cheese plays a significant role in Italian cuisine. Fresh mozzarella (left) marries smooth, creamy texture with milky, mild flavor. Although traditionally made from buffalo's milk, most fresh mozzarella is made with cow's milk. It's stored in a brine, which helps keep it moist. Part-skim mozzarella (right) is a processed cheese with a firmer texture than fresh. Although Caprese salad is usually made with fresh mozzarella, slices of part-skim cheese make a fine substitute and help reduce the fat in the recipe. The firm slices also make an attractive presentation.

The acidity of vine-ripened tomatoes, the mellow sweetness of mozzarella cheese, and the refreshing, slightly minty flavor of fresh basil harmonize in this simple salad. For the best flavor, let the salad come to room temperature before serving. Serve with a side of crusty bread to soak up the juices that remain on the bottom of the plate. This colorful presentation from the island of Capri will add visual intrigue to your seasonal table, delighting both the eye and the palate.

Spaghetti Alla Norma

2 tablespoons olive oil
3 garlic cloves, minced
1½ pounds coarsely chopped peeled tomato (about 2 cups)
1 teaspoon salt
1 pound eggplant, peeled and cut into ½-inch cubes (about 4 cups)
¼ cup thinly sliced fresh basil
¾ pound uncooked spaghetti
6 ounces fresh mozzarella cheese, cut into ¼-inch cubes (about 1 cup)

1. Place oil and garlic in a large skillet; cook over medium-high heat 30 seconds or until garlic begins to sizzle. Add tomato and salt; cook 15 minutes or until liquid evaporates. Add eggplant; cover, reduce heat, and cook 15 minutes or until eggplant is tender. Stir in basil, and set aside. **2.** While sauce simmers, cook pasta in boiling water 9 minutes; drain. Toss with sauce and mozzarella cheese. Serve immediately. Yield: 7 servings (serving size: 1 cup).

CALORIES 329 (29% from fat); FAT 10.5g (sat 3.9g, mono 4.6g, poly 1g); PROTEIN 12.2g; CARB 47.3g; FIBER 4.1g; CHOL 19mg; IRON 2.8mg; SODIUM 444mg; CALC 149mg

Eggplant—the most widely eaten vegetable in Sicily next to the tomato—can be found all over the island from June through September at just about every ristorante, trattoria, osteria, and pizzeria. Look for eggplant at its peak season in American markets during the same timeframe. Fresh eggplant has a sparkling jewel-like color with shiny, smooth skin. It should feel heavy in your hand and be firm but slightly springy. The skin of eggplant is edible, but for this recipe we recommend peeling the vegetable using a sharp knife; afterward, cut it into slices and then cubes.

Sicilian legend reveals that this traditional eggplant pasta dish was renamed Spaghetti Alla Norma after the opera Norma by composer Vincenzo Bellini. The combination of eggplant and tomato in this pasta sauce is quintessentially Sicilian, and it begs to be served with a classic Sicilian wine. Since these can be difficult to find, opt for another variety of bold, spicy red wine with warm Mediterranean flavors such as Librandi's Ciro from the southern province of Calabria.

Spring Risotto

6 cups boiling water, divided
1 cup dried morels
2 pounds unshelled fava beans
5 cups fat-free, less-sodium chicken broth
1 tablespoon olive oil
2 cups thinly sliced leek (about 3 large)
2 garlic cloves, minced
2 cups Arborio rice
2 tablespoons sun-dried tomato paste
1 cup dry white wine
¾ teaspoon salt
½ teaspoon freshly ground black pepper
⅓ cup sliced green onions
¾ cup (3 ounces) finely shredded fresh Romano cheese

1. Combine 3 cups boiling water and morels; cover and let stand 30 minutes. Drain; rinse with cold water. Drain and chop.

2. Remove beans from pods; discard pods. Place beans in a medium saucepan with remaining 3 cups boiling water; cook 1 minute. Drain and rinse with cold water. Drain; remove outer skins from beans. Discard skins.

3. Bring broth to a simmer in a medium saucepan (do not boil). Keep broth warm over low heat.

4. Heat oil in a large saucepan over medium-high heat. Add leek and garlic, and sauté 2 minutes or until leek is tender. Add rice and tomato paste; cook 2 minutes, stirring constantly. Stir in wine, salt, and pepper; cook 1½ minutes or until liquid is absorbed. Stir in 1 cup broth; cook about 2½ minutes or until liquid is nearly absorbed, stirring constantly. Add remaining broth, 1 cup at a time, stirring constantly until each portion is absorbed before adding the next (about 20 minutes total). Stir in morels and beans; cook 30 seconds or until thoroughly heated. Stir in green onions. Sprinkle each serving with cheese. Yield: 8 servings (serving size: 1 cup risotto and 1½ tablespoons cheese).

CALORIES 238 (22% from fat); FAT 5.9g (sat 2.2g, mono 2.9g, poly 0.4g); PROTEIN 9.9g; CARB 29.7g; FIBER 1.6g; CHOL 11mg; IRON 2.6mg; SODIUM 648mg; CALC 135mg

Fava beans (sometimes called broad beans) are actually a member of the pea family and boast a buttery texture with nutty flavor. They must be shelled twice. To remove them from their pods, pull downward on the stem at the top of the bean, separating the sides like a zipper. Then, open the pod with your thumbs and forefingers, and push the beans out. Next, blanch the beans, cool them slightly, and pinch to remove the outer skins. Fresh beans taste the best, but canned fava beans will also work when fresh are out of season.

Risotto is an Italian specialty that's dominant in the northern regions of the country. It's usually made with Italian Arborio rice because of its high starch content and firm texture. Each medium-length grain has a white "eye" that remains firm to the bite, while the rest of the grain softens and lends creaminess to the dish. Risotto can be simply flavored with butter and cheese for a side dish or can become a hearty meal. Fresh fava beans are a sign of spring in Italy, and here they add bright flavor and vibrant color, a fitting balance to earthy morels and a sprinkling of pungent Romano cheese.

Polenta with Bolognese Sauce

Polenta is extraordinarily versatile. Although most often served as a first course, it can also be used as a side dish, main course, or even dessert. Polenta can be cooked in water or broth, or a combination of water and milk or broth and milk. Once cooked, the polenta in this recipe is then pressed into an 8-inch square baking dish. After standing 10 minutes, it's inverted onto a cutting board and cut into four squares. Each square is then cut diagonally forming two triangles. The result is a fancy-looking triangle that's ready for a rich, hearty bolognese sauce.

Sauce:
Cooking spray
- 1 cup finely chopped onion
- ¼ cup finely chopped carrot
- ¾ pound ground round
- 3 garlic cloves, minced
- ⅓ cup dry red wine
- ¼ teaspoon salt
- ¼ teaspoon fennel seeds
- ¼ teaspoon freshly ground black pepper
- 1 (28-ounce) can diced tomatoes, undrained

Polenta:
- 1½ cups 1% reduced-fat milk
- ½ teaspoon salt
- 1 (14-ounce) can fat-free, less-sodium chicken broth
- 1 cup instant polenta
- ½ cup (2 ounces) finely shredded fresh Romano or Parmesan cheese, divided
- ¼ cup chopped fresh basil

1. To prepare sauce, heat a large nonstick skillet over medium-high heat. Coat pan with cooking spray. Add onion, carrot, beef, and garlic; cook 6 minutes or until beef is browned, stirring to crumble. Add wine; cook 1 minute. Add ¼ teaspoon salt, fennel, pepper, and tomatoes. Bring to a boil; cover, reduce heat, and simmer 40 minutes.

2. To prepare polenta, combine milk, ½ teaspoon salt, and broth in a medium saucepan. Gradually add polenta, stirring constantly with a whisk; bring to a boil. Reduce heat to medium; cook 3 minutes or until thick, stirring constantly. Stir in 6 tablespoons cheese.

3. Spoon polenta into an 8-inch square baking dish coated with cooking spray, spreading evenly. Let stand 10 minutes or until firm. Loosen edges of polenta with a knife. Invert polenta onto a cutting board, and cut into 4 squares. Cut each square diagonally into 2 triangles. Place 1 triangle on each of 8 plates; top each serving with ½ cup sauce, ¾ teaspoon cheese, and 1½ teaspoons basil. Yield: 8 servings.

CALORIES 263 (30% from fat); FAT 8.8g (sat 3.8g, mono 3g, poly 0.3g); PROTEIN 15.9g; CARB 28.6g; FIBER 3.7g; CHOL 38mg; IRON 2mg; SODIUM 604mg; CALC 183mg

These polenta triangles offer a change of pace from the traditional pasta and sauce dish. You can make both the sauce and polenta ahead and reheat before serving. To warm the polenta triangles, heat a large nonstick skillet over medium-high heat. Coat the pan with cooking spray. Add the polenta triangles and cook 4 minutes or until lightly browned on the bottom.

Classic Pesto

2 tablespoons coarsely chopped pine nuts or walnuts
2 garlic cloves, peeled
3 tablespoons extravirgin olive oil
4 cups basil leaves (about 4 ounces)
½ cup (2 ounces) grated fresh Parmesan cheese
¼ teaspoon salt

1. Drop nuts and garlic through food chute with food processor on; process until minced. Add oil; pulse 3 times. Add basil, cheese, and salt; process until finely minced, scraping sides of bowl once. Yield: ¾ cup (serving size: 1 tablespoon).

CALORIES 58 (82% from fat); FAT 5.3g (sat 1.3g, mono 3g, poly 0.8g); PROTEIN 2.1g; CARB 0.9g; FIBER 0.6g; CHOL 3mg; IRON 0.5mg; SODIUM 125mg; CALC 72mg

Pine nuts are the pearly seeds from the cones of certain pine trees that are harvested throughout the Mediterranean and across much of Asia. In American markets, most pine nuts are imported from Italy or China because domestic pine trees don't produce the same quality product as those found further east. Pine nuts, or *pignolias*, married with basil make the foundation of a good pesto. They also play a significant role in Italian baking and cooking in general. But pine nuts alone can also be a good-for-you snack, as they're high in the "good" fats. Because of this high-fat content, they can turn rancid easily, so store them in the freezer up to nine months.

Fresh from the stem, basil adds zing to crostini, a simple green salad, or a cool summer soup or pasta. But when fresh basil is turned into pesto—the Italian sauce complete with nuts, Parmesan, garlic, and olive oil—you have a culinary masterpiece. Making pesto is easy, and you don't have to stick to a particular recipe. Experiment by adding sun-dried tomatoes to the basic recipe or substituting another kind of nut. Prepare extra batches and freeze them so you'll have enough pesto to last through the winter. Add sophistication to simple dishes as you toss the bold sauce with penne pasta or use it on top of pizza, chili, or omelets. Try it in mayonnaise to enliven a sandwich of roasted red bell peppers, tomato, and feta; or drop a spoonful or two into tomato-and-chickpea soup.

Veal Marsala

¼ cup all-purpose flour, divided
⅔ cup beef consommé
1 pound veal cutlets
1 tablespoon butter, divided
½ cup dry Marsala wine
1 cup presliced mushrooms
¼ teaspoon salt
4 cups hot cooked vermicelli (about 8 ounces uncooked pasta)

1. Combine 1 tablespoon flour and consommé, stirring with a whisk; set aside. Dredge veal in remaining 3 tablespoons flour. Discard any remaining flour.
2. Melt 1½ teaspoons butter in a large nonstick skillet over medium-high heat. Add half of veal; cook 1½ minutes. Turn veal over; cook 1 minute. Remove veal from pan. Repeat procedure with remaining butter and cutlets.
3. Add wine to pan, scraping pan to loosen browned bits. Add consommé mixture, mushrooms, and salt; bring to a boil. Reduce heat; simmer 3 minutes or until thick. Return veal to pan, turning once to coat well with sauce. Serve with pasta. Yield: 4 servings (serving size: 3 ounces veal, about 2 tablespoons sauce, and 1 cup pasta).

CALORIES 406 (13% from fat); FAT 5.9g (sat 2.6g, mono 1.5g, poly 0.8g); PROTEIN 34g; CARB 48.6g; FIBER 2.7g; CHOL 95mg; IRON 3.4mg; SODIUM 512mg; CALC 20mg

Meat and vegetables are sometimes lightly coated in flour, cornmeal, or breadcrumbs, a process called dredging, to ensure even browning during frying. To dredge veal cutlets in flour, place the flour in a shallow dish such as a pie plate or a baking dish. Drag the meat through the flour, making sure that the cutlets have an even dusting of flour on both sides. Gently shake the cutlets to remove excess flour.

Vitello al marsala, *or veal marsala, is a regional specialty of Sicilian origin. The popular mushroom and wine–based sauce is primarily flavored with Marsala, a dry, dark, and strong fortified wine that gets its name from the town in which the grapes are grown. Serve over vermicelli, linguine, egg noodles, or a blend of white and wild rice.*

Herbed Focaccia

All-Purpose Pizza Dough (recipe
  on page 139)
  1 tablespoon chopped fresh
    flat-leaf parsley
  1 teaspoon dried rubbed sage
  1 teaspoon dried rosemary
  1 teaspoon dried thyme
Cooking spray
  1 tablespoon yellow cornmeal
  1 tablespoon extravirgin
    olive oil
  ½ teaspoon kosher salt

1. Roll prepared dough into a 12 x 8–inch rectangle on a floured surface. Sprinkle parsley, sage, rosemary, and thyme over dough. Fold dough into thirds. Knead lightly 1 minute or until herbs are blended into dough. Cover and let stand 10 minutes. Roll dough into a 14 x 12–inch rectangle. Place dough on a baking sheet coated with cooking spray and sprinkled with cornmeal. Cover and let rise in a warm place 35 minutes or until doubled in size.
2. Preheat oven to 450°.
3. Uncover dough. Make indentations in top of dough using the handle of a wooden spoon or your fingertips. Gently brush dough with oil. Sprinkle with kosher salt. Bake dough at 450° for 15 minutes or until browned. Yield: 8 servings (serving size: 1 slice).

CALORIES 209 (11% from fat); FAT 2.5g (sat 0.4g, mono 1.4g, poly 0.5g); PROTEIN 5.7g; CARB 40.2g; FIBER 1.8g; CHOL 0mg; IRON 2.9mg; SODIUM 295mg; CALC 16mg

Focaccia (foh-KAH-chee-ah), a bread that traditionally contains a fair amount of olive oil, is "dimpled" after rising, giving it a characteristic appearance. This dimpling is done to relieve bubbling on the surface of the bread and to catch olive oil that's drizzled or brushed on before baking. After the dough has fully risen and is ready to be put in the oven, use the handle of a wooden spoon or your fingertips to make indentations evenly across the surface of the dough.

Ask for focaccia on the Tuscan coast, and you'll get what they call schiacciata *in Florence: a thin loaf of dimpled bread that's brushed with olive oil and sprinkled with salt. Eat it as a snack, as an accompaniment to a soup or salad meal, or as the base for a sandwich. The coarse texture of kosher salt provides a wonderful crunch and salty flavor that's reminiscent of a big, soft pretzel.*

Quick Pizza Margherita

1 (13.8-ounce) can refrigerated pizza crust dough
Cooking spray
1 teaspoon extravirgin olive oil, divided
1 garlic clove, halved
5 plum tomatoes, thinly sliced (about ¾ pound)
1 cup (4 ounces) shredded fresh mozzarella cheese
1 teaspoon balsamic vinegar
½ cup thinly sliced fresh basil
⅛ teaspoon salt
⅛ teaspoon black pepper

1. Preheat oven to 400°.
2. Unroll dough onto a baking sheet coated with cooking spray; pat into a 13 x 11–inch rectangle. Bake at 400° for 8 minutes. Remove crust from oven, and brush with ½ teaspoon oil. Rub crust with cut sides of garlic.
3. Arrange tomato slices on crust, leaving a ½-inch border, and sprinkle evenly with cheese. Bake at 400° for 12 minutes or until cheese melts and crust is golden.
4. Combine remaining ½ teaspoon oil and vinegar, stirring with a whisk.
5. Sprinkle pizza evenly with sliced basil, salt, and pepper. Drizzle vinegar mixture evenly over pizza. Cut pizza into 8 pieces. Yield: 4 servings (serving size: 2 pieces).
Note: If you're having trouble shaping the dough, let it rest 5 minutes, and it will become more elastic.

CALORIES 353 (27% from fat); FAT 11g (sat 4.5g, mono 0.9g, poly 0.2g); PROTEIN 16.4g; CARB 52.3g; FIBER 1.2g; CHOL 15mg; IRON 3.3mg; SODIUM 958mg; CALC 214mg

A serrated knife with its scalloped, toothlike edge, is best for cutting through the resistant skin and juicy flesh of a ripe tomato without crushing it. Plum tomatoes have a lower water content than other varieties, making them firmer and easier to cut into thin slices. They also have fewer seeds and are the best year-round tomato, making them the ideal topping to quench pizza cravings any time of the year.

Pizza Margherita, the most popular pizza in present-day Italy, was first made by Neapolitan baker Raffaele Esposito in 1889 in honor of Queen Margherita. It boasts Italy's national colors of red, white, and green, as seen in the flag. Baking the dough before topping it with tomato keeps the crust crisp. Be sure to use fresh mozzarella, which comes packed in water and can be found with other gourmet cheeses.

Frittata with Smoked Cheese and Pancetta

Pancetta, pronounced pan-CHEH-tuh, is an Italian bacon cured with salt, pepper, and other spices, rather than smoked. While American bacon adds a salty-sweet smokiness to a dish, pancetta lends piquant flavor to soups, sauces, meats, and vegetables. Look in your grocery's deli section for salami-like rolls, ready for slicing or chopping. You can also find it prepackaged in thin slices.

Cooking spray
1½ cups frozen Southern-style hash brown potatoes (such as Ore-Ida)
½ cup chopped onion
⅓ cup chopped pancetta (about 2 ounces)
½ teaspoon salt
½ teaspoon hot pepper sauce (such as Tabasco)
⅛ teaspoon black pepper
4 large eggs
4 large egg whites
¼ cup (1 ounce) shredded smoked mozzarella cheese
2 tablespoons chopped green onions
Green onion strips (optional)

1. Preheat broiler.
2. Heat a 10-inch ovenproof nonstick skillet over medium-high heat. Coat pan with cooking spray. Add potatoes, onion, and pancetta; sauté 8 minutes or until potatoes are golden brown. Remove from pan. Wipe pan clean with paper towels; recoat with cooking spray. Combine salt, hot pepper sauce, black pepper, eggs, and egg whites in a medium bowl, stirring with a whisk. Stir in potato mixture, cheese, and chopped green onions.
3. Heat pan over medium heat. Pour in egg mixture. Reduce heat to medium-low; cook 3 minutes or until bottom is lightly browned, lifting edges and tilting pan as eggs cook to allow uncooked portion to flow underneath cooked portion.
4. Broil 2 minutes or until top is lightly browned and set. Garnish with green onion strips, if desired. Yield: 4 servings (serving size: 1 wedge).

CALORIES 198 (50% from fat); FAT 11.1g (sat 4.5g, mono 1.9g, poly 0.7g); PROTEIN 14.9g; CARB 8.9g; FIBER 0.8g; CHOL 225mg; IRON 1mg; SODIUM 701mg; CALC 86mg

Similar to a French omelet, a frittata is an Italian version that resembles a crustless quiche. However, a frittata is different from an omelet because it's finished under a broiler, cut into wedges, and left unfolded during the cooking process. Four eggs, four egg whites, potatoes, pancetta, and smoked cheese go into this frittata, which makes it a particularly satisfying supper.

Instant Tiramisu

1¼ cups part-skim ricotta
    cheese
  1 (8-ounce) block ⅓-less-fat
    cream cheese
  ½ cup sugar
24 ladyfingers (2 [3-ounce]
    packages)
  ½ cup Kahlúa (coffee-flavored
    liqueur)
  1 tablespoon unsweetened
    cocoa

1. Place ricotta cheese, cream cheese, and sugar in a food processor; process until smooth.

2. Arrange 24 ladyfinger halves in a single layer in an 11 x 7–inch baking dish. Drizzle with ¼ cup Kahlúa, and let stand 5 minutes. Spread half of cheese mixture evenly over ladyfingers. Repeat procedure with remaining ladyfingers, Kahlúa, and cheese mixture. Sprinkle with cocoa. Serve immediately or chill until ready to serve. Yield: 10 servings.

CALORIES 237 (31% from fat); FAT 8.2g (sat 5.1g, mono 0.7g, poly 0.1g); PROTEIN 7.5g; CARB 28.7g; FIBER 0.4g; CHOL 56mg; IRON 0.6mg; SODIUM 263mg; CALC 121mg

One of the signature components of a classic Italian tiramisu is the oblong-shaped sponge cakes that form liqueur-soaked layers and often a decorative border along the dessert's exterior. Ladyfingers originated in eleventh-century France, and the recipe, which hasn't changed much since then, spread and quickly became a favorite of European bakers. Find ladyfingers in the bakery section of your supermarket. Most come already split in half lengthwise, but you can split them yourself with a serrated knife, if needed. Substitute sponge cake, brioche, or angel food cake if ladyfingers aren't available.

A perfect Italian meal deserves a perfect Italian dessert—tiramisu. This quick pick-me-up (that's what "tiramisu" means) is lightened by substituting ricotta and cream cheese for the super-rich mascarpone that fills most traditional versions. If you're short on time and long in the sweet tooth, then this instant indulgence is the ideal choice.

antipasti, soup & salad

Minted Prosciutto and Melon

½ cup sweet Italian sparkling
  white wine (such as
  spumante) or sparkling white
  grape juice
1 tablespoon minced fresh
  mint
1 tablespoon honey
24 (1½-inch) cubes ripe
  cantaloupe
6 very thin slices prosciutto
  (about 3 ounces), cut in half
  crosswise, then lengthwise

1. Combine first 4 ingredients in a large bowl, tossing gently to coat. Cover and chill 30 minutes.
2. Remove cantaloupe, reserving wine syrup. Wrap cantaloupe pieces with prosciutto; secure with a wooden pick. Serve with wine syrup for dipping. Yield: 6 servings (serving size: 4 pieces cantaloupe and 4 teaspoons wine mixture).

CALORIES 101 (16% from fat); FAT 1.8g (sat 0.6g, mono 0g, poly 0.1g); PROTEIN 5.3g; CARB 14.8g; FIBER 0.1g; CHOL 8mg; IRON 0.7mg; SODIUM 276mg; CALC 16mg

When selecting a cantaloupe, forget about shaking and thumping the melon. Rather, put your nose to the test by searching for a sweet-smelling melon with thick netting and a golden (not green) undertone. The stem end should have a small indentation; a small crack is a sign of sweetness, but make sure to avoid any melon with mold. Store a ripe cantaloupe in the refrigerator for no more than five days.

Transparently thin slices of salty prosciutto wrapped gingerly around a juicy chunk of cubed orange-hued melon is a modern antipasto indulgence. Its roots, however, date back to the Roman custom in classical times of pairing melon or figs with prosciutto di Parma. A quick soak in sweet wine, honey, and mint is all the melon needs—any longer and it begins to dilute the flavors.

Grilled Vegetable Antipasto

2 red bell peppers
2 zucchini (about 1 pound),
   each cut in half lengthwise
2 small eggplant (about
   8 ounces), each quartered
   lengthwise
¼ cup chopped fresh parsley
¼ cup balsamic vinegar
1 tablespoon extravirgin
   olive oil
¼ teaspoon salt
6 garlic cloves, peeled and
   crushed

1. Prepare grill.
2. Place peppers on grill rack; grill 15 minutes or until charred, turning occasionally. Remove peppers from grill. Place peppers in a zip-top plastic bag; seal and let stand 15 minutes. Peel peppers; cut peppers in half lengthwise, and discard seeds and membranes. Coarsely chop peppers; place in a large zip-top plastic bag. Place zucchini and eggplant on grill rack; grill 10 minutes, turning occasionally. Remove zucchini and eggplant from grill; let stand 10 minutes. Coarsely chop zucchini and eggplant; add to chopped peppers.
3. Combine parsley and remaining 4 ingredients, stirring with a whisk. Pour parsley mixture over pepper mixture. Seal bag; toss gently to coat. Refrigerate at least 2 hours or overnight. Yield: 4 servings (serving size: 1 cup).

CALORIES 122 (30% from fat); FAT 4g (sat 0.6g, mono 2.5g, poly 0.6g); PROTEIN 3.9g; CARB 21.1g; FIBER 6.7g; CHOL 0mg; IRON 1.7mg; SODIUM 163mg; CALC 52mg

While there are many ways to remove the skin from a bell pepper, all methods involve charring or slightly cooking the outside of the pepper. The method used in this particular recipe is grilling. Grilling the bell pepper creates an air pocket, thus separating the skin from the flesh. Once grilled, place the hot pepper in a zip-top plastic bag. The steam from the charred pepper will help loosen the skin and make peeling it even easier. After 15 minutes in the zip-top bag, remove and peel the pepper. Be sure to discard the charred skin; it isn't used in the recipe.

Colorful grilled and marinated vegetables are the stars of this antipasto—"before the pasta"—plate. Though antipasto usually precedes a pasta dish, it isn't imperative. This particular antipasto plate will complement a wide range of meals. Grilling the zucchini and the eggplant makes them more absorbent, allowing them to soak up the vinaigrette.

Marinated Olives

24 large unpitted Spanish olives
2 tablespoons sherry vinegar
1 tablespoon extravirgin
　olive oil
2 teaspoons coriander seeds,
　crushed
1 teaspoon dried thyme
1 teaspoon dried rosemary,
　crushed
½ teaspoon crushed red
　pepper
2 garlic cloves, thinly sliced
Rosemary sprigs (optional)

1. Combine first 8 ingredients in a bowl. Cover and marinate in refrigerator at least 8 hours, stirring occasionally. Serve at room temperature. Garnish with rosemary sprigs, if desired. Yield: 6 servings (serving size: 4 olives).

CALORIES 49 (66% from fat); FAT 3.6g (sat 0.1g, mono 2g, poly 1.4g); PROTEIN 0.2g; CARB 3.1g; FIBER 0.2g; CHOL 0mg; IRON 0.4mg; SODIUM 322mg; CALC 13mg

A mortar and pestle are the best tools for crushing spices, and many people think this method releases a better, gentler flavor than using a spice grinder. We agree, and recommend using a mortar and pestle to crush the coriander seeds and the rosemary in this marinated olive recipe. A small, deep mortar is better than a wide, shallow one, from which the spices tend to shoot out. However, if you don't have a mortar and pestle on hand, consider using a meat mallet or rolling pin. Remember: the finer you crush the spices, the more powerful and pervasive their effect on the finished dish.

Most olives in Italy are destined to be pressed into oil; however, there are others—green and black varieties—that will make it directly to the Mediterranean table. Whether they're served on their own, as in this marinated dish, or become a garnish or topping for pizza or crostini, olives certainly make a profound flavor impact. Serve these olives with a pinot noir for a perfect addition to a supper club spread. You can make and refrigerate this dish up to a week ahead, freeing you up for last-minute party preparations. The flavors actually improve as the olives marinate.

Eggplant Caponata

Oil and vinegar are an ideal pair; the tartness of the vinegar is subdued by the smoothness of the oil, making them the base upon which many salad dressings are built. Simple oil-and-vinegar dressings, however, aren't confined to the salad bowl. In fact, these two ingredients add the same complimentary smooth tartness to stovetop dishes, as in this caponata.

6 cups diced peeled eggplant (about 1 pound)
1½ teaspoons salt
¼ cup golden raisins
4 teaspoons olive oil, divided
1 cup chopped onion
2 garlic cloves, minced
1 cup diced seeded plum tomato
¼ cup sugar
¼ cup red wine vinegar
¼ cup chopped pitted kalamata olives
2 teaspoons capers
⅓ cup chopped fresh parsley

1. Place eggplant in a colander; sprinkle with salt. Toss well. Drain 1 hour. Rinse well; pat dry with paper towels.
2. Place raisins in a small bowl; cover with hot water. Let stand 15 minutes; drain. Set aside.
3. Heat 1 tablespoon oil in a large nonstick skillet over medium-high heat. Add eggplant; sauté 9 minutes or until well browned. Spoon eggplant into a large bowl; set aside.
4. Heat 1 teaspoon oil in pan over medium-high heat. Add onion; sauté 3 minutes or until golden. Add garlic; sauté 1 minute. Add tomato; sauté 2 minutes. Add tomato mixture to eggplant, tossing gently to combine.
5. Return pan to heat. Add sugar and vinegar, stirring until sugar dissolves. Stir in raisins, olives, and capers. Add eggplant mixture, stirring to combine. Remove from heat; stir in parsley. Serve warm or at room temperature. Yield: 12 servings (serving size: ¼ cup).

Note: Caponata will keep in the refrigerator up to five days; bring to room temperature before serving.

CALORIES 59 (31% from fat); FAT 2g (sat 0.3g, mono 1.4g, poly 0.2g); PROTEIN 0.8g; CARB 10.8g; FIBER 1.5g; CHOL 0mg; IRON 0.5mg; SODIUM 141mg; CALC 14mg

The late James Beard, considered to be the godfather of American cuisine, once said, "Nothing but the best is good enough for friends." If that's your motto, then Eggplant Caponata is a sure-serve for your next cocktail party. Caponata (kap-oh-NAH-tah) is an eggplant-based dish that can be served as an antipasto or a condiment, or alongside chicken, pork, or fish. Salty, acidic red wine vinegar, tomatoes, capers, and kalamata olives harmonize with sugar and golden raisins, creating a sweet-and-sour taste that's frequently found in Sicilian cooking. Though most often served at room temperature, it's also good warm or chilled. Simply remove the caponata from the refrigerator 30 minutes before your guests arrive. For an appetizer, serve the caponata with a slice of toasted Italian bread.

Tomato Crostini

½ cup chopped plum tomato
1 tablespoon chopped fresh basil
1 tablespoon chopped pitted green olives
1 teaspoon capers
½ teaspoon balsamic vinegar
½ teaspoon olive oil
⅛ teaspoon sea salt
Dash of freshly ground black pepper
1 garlic clove, minced
4 (1-inch-thick) slices French bread baguette
Cooking spray
1 garlic clove, halved

1. Preheat oven to 375°.
2. Combine first 9 ingredients.
3. Lightly coat both sides of bread slices with cooking spray, and arrange bread slices in a single layer on a baking sheet. Bake at 375° for 4 minutes on each side or until lightly toasted.
4. Rub 1 side of each bread slice with cut side of garlic; top with tomato mixture. Yield: 2 servings (serving size: 2 bread slices and about ⅓ cup tomato mixture).

CALORIES 109 (23% from fat); FAT 2.8g (sat 0.4g, mono 1.5g, poly 0.7g); PROTEIN 3.1g; CARB 18g; FIBER 1.4g; CHOL 0mg; IRON 1mg; SODIUM 373mg; CALC 30mg

There are few greater pleasures than a just-picked, or just-chopped, ripe red tomato—especially plum tomatoes. Plum tomatoes, also called Roma or Italian, are an egg-shaped variety that can be either yellow or red. Though not as sweet or acidic as beefsteak or globe varieties, the plum tomato has a lower water content and fewer seeds, so they're especially good for cooking and canning. Plum tomatoes are the best year-round supermarket tomatoes and are what we prefer for Tomato Crostini.

Crostini, which actually means "little crusts," is an integral part of Italian culture and cuisine. Toasted bread slices topped with vibrant red chopped plum tomatoes are popular throughout the Mediterranean region.

Minestrone Bowl

Sun-dried tomatoes add a burst of vivid flavor and nutrition to many dishes, including this Minestrone Bowl. When dried, the naturally sweet taste of Roma, or plum, tomatoes intensifies. Their slightly chewy texture adds richness to the consistency of a dish. To rehydrate dry-packed tomatoes, place them in a bowl with boiling water; allow them to soak for 30 minutes to soften their texture.

½ cup sun-dried tomatoes (packed without oil)
2 cups boiling water
1 tablespoon olive oil
2 cups chopped less-sodium ham
2 cups chopped onion
1 cup chopped carrot
1 cup chopped celery
5 garlic cloves, chopped
6 cups water
1 (14.5-ounce) can diced tomatoes, undrained
1 zucchini, halved lengthwise and sliced
1 (16-ounce) can cannellini beans or other white beans, rinsed and drained
¼ cup chopped fresh basil
¼ teaspoon salt
¾ teaspoon black pepper
3½ cups hot cooked linguine (about 7 ounces uncooked pasta)
¼ cup plus 2 teaspoons (about 1 ounce) grated fresh Parmesan cheese

1. Combine sun-dried tomatoes and boiling water in a bowl; let stand 30 minutes. Drain sun-dried tomatoes through a sieve into a bowl, reserving soaking liquid. Cut sun-dried tomatoes into julienne strips.

2. Heat olive oil in a large Dutch oven over medium-high heat. Add sun-dried tomatoes, ham, and next 4 ingredients, and sauté 5 minutes. Add reserved soaking liquid, 6 cups water, and diced tomatoes; bring to a boil. Cover, reduce heat, and simmer 30 minutes. Add zucchini and beans; cook 5 minutes. Stir in basil, salt, and pepper. Place pasta into large shallow bowls; top with broth mixture and cheese. Yield: 7 servings (serving size: ½ cup pasta, 2 cups broth mixture, and 2 teaspoons cheese).

CALORIES 319 (21% from fat); FAT 7.4g (sat 2.1g, mono 3.3g, poly 1.4g); PROTEIN 17.1g; CARB 48.1g; FIBER 5.5g; CHOL 22mg; IRON 4mg; SODIUM 822mg; CALC 139mg

The supertrend of big Asian noodle bowls has literally spilled over into other cuisines around the world. We see that trend here in this Italian-with-a-twist minestrone (mee-ness-TROH-nay). Minestrone is an Italian vegetable soup made with pasta and beans. The most common pasta is broken spaghetti, ditalini, or other tubular varieties. Here, we've chosen linguine which makes this recipe a cross between a true minestrone and an Asian noodle bowl. The dish is thick enough to be considered a one-course meal, and is topped with a sprinkling of Parmesan cheese which is, of course, an Italian tradition. Because liquid is such a great carrier of aromas and tastes, our oversized serving is intensely flavored with tomatoes, garlic, and Italian seasonings.

Tuscan White
Bean Soup with Prosciutto

2 teaspoons olive oil
½ cup chopped prosciutto or
  ham (about 2 ounces)
1 cup chopped onion
¾ cup chopped celery
¾ cup chopped carrot
1 garlic clove, minced
1 cup water
2 (19-ounce) cans cannellini
  beans or other white beans,
  undrained
1 (14-ounce) can fat-free,
  less-sodium chicken broth
2 bay leaves
2 tablespoons minced fresh
  parsley
2 tablespoons sherry (optional)
¼ teaspoon black pepper

1. Heat oil in a large stockpot over medium heat. Add chopped prosciutto, and sauté 2 minutes. Add chopped onion, celery, carrot, and minced garlic; sauté 2 minutes or until soft.
2. Add 1 cup water, beans, broth, and bay leaves, and bring soup to a boil. Partially cover, reduce heat, and simmer 20 minutes.
3. Add parsley, sherry, if desired, and pepper; cook 1 minute. Discard bay leaves. Yield: 4 servings (serving size: 1½ cups).

CALORIES 292 (14% from fat); FAT 4.7g (sat 0.8g, mono 2.3g, poly 1.5g); PROTEIN 15.9g; CARB 45.3g; FIBER 12g; CHOL 8mg; IRON 4.3mg; SODIUM 1,095mg; CALC 114mg

The best *prosciutto* (proh-SHOO-toh) sold in the United States comes from the Parma area of Italy; it's made from larger pork legs than American prosciutto and is aged longer. It also isn't smoked like American ham; rather, it's air-cured with salt and seasonings pressed into a densely-textured meat. It's typically sliced thin and eaten raw or lightly cooked. Domestic prosciutto is fine for flavoring sauces, soups, and stews, but when you're really spotlighting the ham, go for *prosciutto di Parma.* In Italy, it's considered the ultimate indulgence.

White bean soup is a quintessential Tuscan dish. Traditionally a meatless soup, it's made as a tribute to the Italian's beloved white bean. To add depth of flavor, however, we've added prosciutto—another Italian favorite. The canned beans allow you to prepare this soup in just over 30 minutes. However, the sodium is high, especially since the beans aren't drained and rinsed. For a low-sodium soup, cook your own dried beans. While the soup is simmering, assemble a salad and toast some Italian bread.

Beet and Fennel Soup

4 beets (about 1 pound)
¼ cup water
1 large onion (about 1 pound)
4 cups organic vegetable
 broth (such as Swanson
 Certified Organic)
1¾ cups chopped fennel bulb
 (about 1 large)
1 cup chopped peeled Granny
 Smith apple
2 teaspoons white wine
 vinegar
2 teaspoons lemon juice
½ teaspoon salt
½ teaspoon freshly ground
 black pepper
8 teaspoons reduced-fat sour
 cream
Chopped fennel fronds

Fennel has culinary versatility worth exploring. It's used two ways in this Beet and Fennel Soup. Chopped fennel bulb contributes to the body of the soup, and fennel fronds, the wispy dill-like greenery on top of the fennel bulb, serve as a garnish. Native to the Mediterranean region, fennel is a licorice-flavored member of the parsley family and is one of Italy's most popular vegetables. Fennel is notorious for adding wonderful flavor to Italian soups and tomato sauces. When using fronds, add them near the end of the cooking process so their flavor isn't diluted.

1. Preheat oven to 375°.
2. Leave root and 1 inch of stem on beets; scrub with a brush. Place beets on a large sheet of aluminum foil, and sprinkle beets with ¼ cup water. Wrap beets in foil; arrange packet of beets and onion on a baking sheet. Bake at 375° for 1 hour or until tender. Cool.
3. Combine broth, fennel, and apple in a medium saucepan. Bring to a boil; reduce heat, and simmer 15 minutes or until fennel is tender. Cool.
4. Trim off beet roots; rub off skins, and coarsely chop. Peel and quarter onion. Add beets and onion to broth mixture, stirring to combine. Place half of beet mixture in a blender; process until smooth. Pour pureed beet mixture into a large bowl. Repeat procedure with remaining beet mixture. Stir in vinegar, juice, salt, and pepper. Return beet mixture to pan.
5. Place beet mixture over medium heat, and cook 2 minutes or until thoroughly heated. Ladle soup into bowls, and top with sour cream. Sprinkle evenly with fennel fronds. Yield: 8 servings (serving size: ¾ cup soup and 1 teaspoon sour cream).

CALORIES 74 (11% from fat); FAT 0.9g (sat 0.4g, mono 0.2g, poly 0.1g); PROTEIN 2.2g; CARB 15.3g; FIBER 3.3g; CHOL 2mg; IRON 0.8mg; SODIUM 496mg; CALC 42mg

Showcase autumn's best produce with this vermillion-hued soup, which balances sweet oven-baked beets with the sharpness of apple and lemon. Baking the beets concentrates their flavor; the onion is roasted whole. Fennel, which has become one of Italy's most important vegetables, also stars in this sensational soup. Fennel fronds make a nice green garnish atop the milky-white sour cream.

Endive Stuffed with Goat Cheese and Walnuts

A member of the chicory family, Belgian endive is a small, cigar-shaped head of compact, pointed leaves that's grown in complete darkness. The leaves are creamy white with pale yellow-green or red tips. The red-tipped variety is believed to be a mutation of the original yellow-green variety, and is found primarily in the United States; it may be substituted in this recipe if you prefer. Belgian endive has a slightly bitter flavor and crunchy leaves that are perfect for stuffing, scooping, or dipping. Wrap any leftover leaves in a dry paper towel to prevent overexposure to light, and refrigerate for up to five days.

⅓ cup coarsely chopped walnuts
2 tablespoons honey, divided
Cooking spray
¼ cup balsamic vinegar
3 tablespoons orange juice
16 Belgian endive leaves (about 2 heads)
16 small orange sections (about 2 navel oranges)
⅓ cup (1½ ounces) crumbled goat cheese or blue cheese
1 tablespoon minced fresh chives
¼ teaspoon cracked black pepper

1. Preheat oven to 350°.
2. Combine walnuts and 1 tablespoon honey; spread on a baking sheet coated with cooking spray. Bake at 350° for 10 minutes, stirring after 5 minutes.
3. Combine 1 tablespoon honey, vinegar, and orange juice in a small saucepan. Bring mixture to a boil over high heat, and cook until reduced to 3 tablespoons (about 5 minutes).
4. Fill each endive leaf with 1 orange section. Top each section with 1 teaspoon cheese and 1 teaspoon walnuts; arrange on a plate. Drizzle vinegar mixture evenly over leaves, and sprinkle evenly with chives and pepper. Yield: 8 servings (serving size: 2 stuffed leaves).

CALORIES 92 (44% from fat); FAT 4.5g (sat 1.1g, mono 0.7g, poly 2.4g); PROTEIN 2.5g; CARB 11.9g; FIBER 2g; CHOL 3mg; IRON 0.6mg; SODIUM 29mg; CALC 43mg

Served as an appetizer or a salad, this dish is a real crowd-pleaser. Every bite packs a contrast of flavors and textures—salty, sweet, tangy, bitter, creamy, and crunchy. Walnuts, which grow abundantly in central and southern Italy, help contribute to the diverse texture. This recipe is a must-have at your next wine-tasting or cocktail party.

Caesar Salad with Crisp Croutons

Homemade croutons are a snap to make and well worth the effort. They're more flavorful and fresher than any store-bought brand, and are far more healthful. To prepare, begin by stacking two slices of sourdough or French bread on top of each other, and slice into ½-inch sticks. Then, moving from one end of the pieces to the other, slice the bread in ½-inch increments. Depending on the thickness of the slices you started with, you should end up with ½-inch cubes of bread. Now you're ready to continue with the Crisp Croutons recipe.

¼ cup egg substitute
1 tablespoon fresh lemon juice
3 tablespoons extravirgin olive oil
3 tablespoons red wine vinegar
1½ teaspoons anchovy paste
1 teaspoon Worcestershire sauce
½ teaspoon freshly ground black pepper
¼ teaspoon fine sea salt
2 garlic cloves, minced
18 cups torn romaine and hearty field greens
2 cups Crisp Croutons
¼ cup (1 ounce) shredded fresh Parmesan cheese

1. Combine egg substitute and juice; gradually add oil, whisking constantly. Stir in vinegar and next 5 ingredients. Place greens, croutons, and cheese in a large bowl. Add dressing; toss well to coat. Yield: 12 servings (serving size 1½ cups).

(Totals include Crisp Croutons) CALORIES 75 (48% from fat); FAT 4.4g (sat 0.9g, mono 2.8g, poly 0.5g); PROTEIN 3g; CARB 6g; FIBER 2g; CHOL 2mg; IRON 2mg; SODIUM 210mg; CALC 63mg

Crisp Croutons

1. Preheat oven to 350°.
2. Combine 6 cups (½-inch) cubed sourdough or French bread; 1 tablespoon butter, melted; 1 teaspoon paprika; and 1 teaspoon onion powder in a jelly-roll pan; toss well. Bake at 350° for 20 minutes or until toasted, turning once. Yield: 6 cups (serving size: ½ cup).

CALORIES 24 (26% from fat); FAT 0.7g (sat 0.4g, mono 0.2g, poly 0.1g); PROTEIN 0.7g; CARB 4g; FIBER 0.2g; CHOL 1mg; IRON 0.2mg; SODIUM 48mg; CALC 6mg

Crispy croutons and Mediterranean flavors make Caesar salad hard to turn down, even if it usually comes with enough fat and cholesterol to fill a Roman coliseum. Not so with this lightened version. Tangy and tasty, it has all the zing of the classic minus the unhealthy elements. Unlike the traditional Caesar salad that sports raw egg—a real food safety no-no—our updated version uses egg substitute which is a pasteurized product.

Panzanella

Olive oil is not only healthier for you than most other oils, it also has a fresh taste, an aromatic smell, and is very versatile. It's primarily used for two purposes: as a fat for cooking and as a condiment for adding flavor to a dish. When used for flavor, extravirgin oil is best. It comes from the first cold pressing of olives. Since neither heat nor chemicals are used in harvesting, the result is a deep olive flavor. Use extravirgin olive oil to make an outstanding vinaigrette, drizzle over bread, or add a finishing touch to just about about any dish.

4 (1-ounce) slices Italian bread
Cooking spray
1 cup torn fresh basil leaves
½ cup thinly sliced red onion
⅓ cup pitted kalamata olives, halved
2 pounds ripe tomatoes, cored and cut into 1-inch pieces
1 (16-ounce) can cannellini beans or other white beans, rinsed and drained
3 tablespoons red wine vinegar
1 tablespoon water
1 tablespoon extravirgin olive oil
1 garlic clove, minced
½ teaspoon freshly ground black pepper
¼ teaspoon salt

1. Preheat oven to 350°.

2. Trim crusts from bread slices; discard crusts. Cut bread into 1-inch cubes. Arrange bread cubes in a single layer on a baking sheet; coat bread with cooking spray. Bake at 350° for 15 minutes or until toasted.

3. Combine basil and next 4 ingredients in a large bowl. Combine vinegar and remaining 5 ingredients in a small bowl; stir with a whisk. Pour over tomato mixture; toss to coat. Add bread cubes; toss well. Serve immediately. Yield: 4 servings (serving size: 2 cups).

CALORIES 255 (29% from fat); FAT 8.1g (sat 1g, mono 4.9g, poly 1.1g); PROTEIN 9.8g; CARB 39.9g; FIBER 8.2g; CHOL 0mg; IRON 3.4mg; SODIUM 708mg; CALC 83mg

Like many Italian dishes, panzanella (pahn-zah-NEHL-lah) was probably first made out of necessity—combining stale bread with readily available fresh garden vegetables. This classic bread salad, full of juicy tomatoes, is like summer on a plate. It's best when the toasted bread is still crisp, so serve immediately after tossing.

pasta, risotto & polenta

Ziti Baked with Spinach, Tomatoes, and Smoked Gouda

Smoked Gouda, with its edible brown rind, creamy yellow interior, and smoky, nutlike flavor, is one of America's favorite Dutch cheeses. We used it in this pasta dish as a substitute for the more traditional Italian favorite—smoked mozzarella. Both cheeses shred easily, melt quickly, and can be added near the end of the cooking time.

8 ounces uncooked ziti
1 tablespoon olive oil
1 cup chopped onion
1 cup chopped yellow bell pepper (about 6 ounces)
3 garlic cloves, minced
1 (14.5-ounce) can diced tomatoes with basil, garlic, and oregano, undrained
1 (10-ounce) can Italian-seasoned diced tomatoes (such as Rotel Bold Italian), undrained
4 cups baby spinach
1¼ cups (5 ounces) shredded smoked Gouda cheese, divided
Cooking spray

1. Cook pasta according to package directions, omitting salt and fat. Drain well.
2. Preheat oven to 375°.
3. Heat oil in a Dutch oven over medium-high heat. Add onion and pepper; sauté 5 minutes. Add garlic; sauté 2 minutes or until onion is tender. Stir in tomatoes; bring to a boil. Reduce heat, and simmer 5 minutes, stirring occasionally. Add spinach to pan; cook 30 seconds or until spinach wilts, stirring frequently. Remove from heat. Add pasta and ¾ cup cheese to tomato mixture, tossing well to combine. Spoon pasta mixture into 5 individual casserole dishes lightly coated with cooking spray; sprinkle evenly with ½ cup cheese. Bake at 375° for 15 minutes or until cheese melts and begins to brown. Yield: 5 servings (serving size: 1 casserole).

CALORIES 382 (30% from fat); FAT 12.7g (sat 5.7g, mono 4.6g, poly 0.9g); PROTEIN 17g; CARB 52.3g; FIBER 4.3g; CHOL 33mg; IRON 4.4mg; SODIUM 977mg; CALC 334mg

This satisfying meatless casserole oozes with al dente tubes of ziti, bright yellow bell peppers, fire-engine red diced tomatoes, tender baby spinach, and smoky shredded Gouda. You can also bake it in an 11 x 7–inch baking dish. Substitute smoked mozzarella for the smoked Gouda for a more authentic Italian dish.

Ricotta Ravioli with Browned Poppy Seed Butter and Asparagus

Ricotta cheese is a fresh, moist Italian cheese that's slightly sweet and can be used in both sweet and savory dishes. It's easy to make, and you'll find the fresh flavor is worth the effort. See pages 140 and 141 for instructions and tips on how to make homemade ricotta cheese. This recipe also calls for ricotta salata, which is different from ricotta cheese. Ricotta salata is a firm, aged cheese with a sharp, slightly sweet flavor; substitute Parmesan if your supermarket doesn't carry it.

Ravioli:
- 1 cup (8 ounces) Homemade Ricotta Cheese (recipe on page 141)
- ¼ cup (1 ounce) grated fresh pecorino Romano cheese
- 2 tablespoons minced fresh flat-leaf parsley
- ⅛ teaspoon salt
- 2 large egg whites
- 48 (3-inch) round gyoza skins
- 6 quarts water

Topping:
- 1½ tablespoons butter
- 2 cups (2-inch) slices asparagus
- ¼ teaspoon salt
- 2 teaspoons poppy seeds
- ⅓ cup (about 1½ ounces) crumbled ricotta salata cheese

1. To prepare ravioli, combine Homemade Ricotta Cheese, pecorino Romano, parsley, ⅛ teaspoon salt, and egg whites; mix with a fork until blended. Working with 1 gyoza skin at a time (cover remaining skins to prevent drying), spoon about 2 teaspoons ricotta mixture into center of skin. Moisten edges of skin with water; place 1 skin over filling, stretching slightly to meet edges of bottom skin. Press edges together with a fork to seal; place on a lightly floured baking sheet (cover with a damp towel to prevent drying). **2.** Bring 6 quarts water to a boil over medium-high heat. Add 4 ravioli; cook 5 minutes, turning ravioli carefully after 2½ minutes. Remove ravioli from water with a slotted spoon; place on a platter. Repeat procedure with remaining ravioli; cover and keep warm. Reserve ½ cup cooking water. **3.** To prepare topping, melt butter in a large nonstick skillet over medium heat; cook 3 minutes or until lightly browned, shaking pan occasionally. Add ¼ cup reserved cooking water, asparagus, and ¼ teaspoon salt; cook 3 minutes or until asparagus is crisp-tender and water evaporates. Stir in poppy seeds; cook 30 seconds. Add remaining ¼ cup reserved cooking water; cook over medium-high heat 1 minute or until liquid is reduced by about half. Add ravioli to pan; toss gently to combine. Sprinkle with ricotta salata; serve immediately. Yield: 6 servings (serving size: 4 ravioli, about ⅓ cup asparagus mixture, and about 1 tablespoon ricotta salata).

CALORIES 356 (30% from fat); FAT 12g (sat 6.6g, mono 2.9g, poly 1.1g); PROTEIN 19.6g; CARB 42.6g; FIBER 2.5g; CHOL 41mg; IRON 3mg; SODIUM 833mg; CALC 288mg

Delicate homemade ricotta cheese creates a smooth filling for ravioli. If you can't find round gyoza skins, cut square wonton wrappers into circles with a 3-inch round cutter.

Spaghetti Carbonara

8 ounces uncooked spaghetti
1 cup chopped cooked ham
⅓ cup (1½ ounces) grated
   Parmigiano-Reggiano or
   Parmesan cheese
¼ cup reduced-fat sour cream
½ teaspoon salt
2 large eggs, lightly beaten
1 garlic clove, minced
¼ teaspoon coarsely ground
   black pepper

1. Cook pasta according to package directions, omitting salt and fat. Drain pasta in a colander over a bowl, reserving ½ cup liquid.

2. Heat a large nonstick skillet over medium heat. Add ham, and cook 2 minutes or until thoroughly heated. Add pasta, and stir well. Combine cheese and next 4 ingredients, stirring with a whisk. Add reserved pasta liquid to egg mixture, stirring with a whisk. Pour egg mixture over pasta mixture; stir well. Cook over low heat 5 minutes or until sauce thickens, stirring constantly (do not boil). Sprinkle with pepper. Serve immediately. Yield: 4 servings (serving size: 1 cup).

CALORIES 352 (25% from fat); FAT 9.6g; (sat 4.6g, mono 2.2g, poly 0.9g); PROTEIN 21g; CARB 45g; FIBER 1.4g; CHOL 139mg; IRON 1.7mg; SODIUM 748mg; CALC 179mg

In a traditional carbonara, the heat from the cooked pasta is sufficient to melt the cheese and cook the egg, leaving the pasta coated with sauce. However, we updated the recipe by lightly beating the eggs, and then combining them with the cheese and sour cream. This procedure allows us to cook the mixture over low heat for a few minutes, ensuring that the eggs are thoroughly cooked. The result is a rich sauce that yields a well-coated pasta.

Carbonara (kar-boh-NAH-rah) literally translates as the "charcoal maker's wife." Word has it that the charcoal sellers from Abruzzo introduced this dish to the city of Rome. For a simple, tasty supper, you can't go wrong with this recipe. And if you have leftover ham it's even better, as chopped ham replaces the bacon in this version of the classic Italian dish. To speed up the prep even more, leave the water for the pasta covered so it will come to a boil faster.

Spaghettini with Oil and Garlic

6 quarts water
2¾ teaspoons salt, divided
1 pound uncooked spaghettini
2 tablespoons extravirgin olive oil
10 garlic cloves, sliced
½ cup chopped fresh flat-leaf parsley
½ teaspoon crushed red pepper
1 cup (4 ounces) grated Parmigiano-Reggiano cheese

1. Bring 6 quarts water and 2 teaspoons salt to a boil in a large stockpot. Stir in pasta; partially cover, and return to a boil, stirring frequently. Cook 6 minutes or until pasta is almost al dente, stirring occasionally. Drain pasta in a colander over a bowl, reserving 1 cup cooking liquid.

2. While pasta cooks, heat oil in a large nonstick skillet over medium heat. Add garlic; cook 2 minutes or until fragrant or beginning to turn golden, stirring constantly. Remove from heat; stir in remaining ¾ teaspoon salt, reserved 1 cup cooking water, parsley, and pepper.

3. Add pasta to pan, stirring well to coat. Return pan to medium heat; cook 1 minute or until pasta is al dente, tossing to coat. Place 1 cup pasta mixture in each of 8 bowls; sprinkle each serving with 2 tablespoons cheese. Serve immediately. Yield: 8 servings.

CALORIES 303 (24% from fat); FAT 8g; (sat 2.9g, mono 3.7g, poly 0.8g); PROTEIN 12.7g; CARB 44.4g; FIBER 1.6g; CHOL 10mg; IRON 2.6mg; SODIUM 603mg; CALC 190mg

Fresh herbs are vital in Italian cooking due to their aromatic flavor and the Italian love affair with pristine ingredients. One of the most commonly used herbs is flat-leaf, or Italian, parsley. A flat-leafed, dark green variety of parsley, it has a strong, robust flavor. Fresh is available year-round, so dried flat-leaf parsley should only be used if you're in a bind. To keep parsley fresh for up to one week, trim about ¼ inch from the stem, and rinse with cold water. Loosely wrap the parsley in a damp paper towel, seal in a zip-top plastic bag filled with air, and refrigerate.

On an Italian menu you will probably find this recipe titled Aglio e Olio (AH-lyoh ay OH-lyoh) meaning "garlic and oil." The dish comes together quickly, so it's a good weeknight dinner. Just pair it with a green salad and a bottle of wine. Spaghettini is in between the sizes of vermicelli and spaghetti, so either of those is a good substitute. Be careful not to overcook the garlic, as browned garlic tastes bitter. Push the garlic to one side of the pan so it will cook evenly.

Linguine with Red Clam Sauce

12 ounces uncooked linguine
2 teaspoons olive oil
2 teaspoons bottled minced garlic
1 (25.5-ounce) bottle fat-free marinara pasta sauce (such as Muir Glen)
2 tablespoons sun-dried or regular tomato paste
¼ teaspoon crushed red pepper
3 (6½-ounce) cans chopped clams, undrained

1. Cook pasta according to package directions, omitting salt and fat. Drain, and keep warm.

2. Heat oil in a medium saucepan over medium heat. Add garlic; sauté 2 minutes. Stir in marinara sauce, tomato paste, and red pepper; bring to a simmer. Drain clams in a sieve over a bowl, reserving liquid; set clams aside. Stir reserved clam liquid into marinara-sauce mixture. Simmer 10 minutes. Stir in clams, and simmer 3 minutes. Serve pasta with sauce. Yield: 6 servings (serving size: 1 cup pasta and about 1 cup sauce).

CALORIES 330 (8% from fat); FAT 3.1g (sat 0.5g, mono 1.4g, poly 0.6); PROTEIN 16.9g; CARB 48.5g; FIBER 3.6g; CHOL 29mg; IRON 6.8mg; SODIUM 833mg; CALC 166mg

Tomato paste is a richly flavored tomato concentrate made from ripened tomatoes that have been cooked for several hours, strained, and reduced. The result is a thick red paste that's perfect for adding hearty flavor to pizza or pasta sauces. When a recipe calls for a small amount of paste, it's convenient to use paste from a tube. However, if you prefer canned paste but don't know what to do with leftover paste, here's a suggestion: Spoon any remaining paste by the tablespoon onto a baking sheet and freeze. Store the frozen paste in a heavy-duty plastic freezer bag. It'll already be measured and ready for your next recipe.

Clams are harvested all over Italy, and Italians in particular like to cook clams in their shells directly in the sauce. We've adapted that custom, however, to fit the American lifestyle of convenience by using canned clams. Stock your pantry properly, and you'll have items on hand for a last-minute dinner. Ready-to-use ingredients such as dried pasta, olive oil, canned clams, tomato paste, bottled garlic, and pasta sauce have you well on your way to a convenient throw-together meal. While both red and white clam sauces are popular throughout Italy, a red sauce is a healthier choice. There are more calories and fat in a white sauce because of the butter and wine base.

Seafood Lasagna

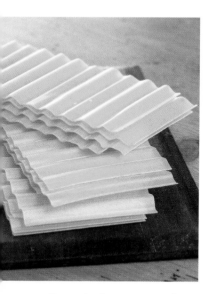

Precooked, or oven-ready, lasagna noodles are a great way to save prep time and effort without sacrificing flavor or texture. Most versions of oven-ready noodles are preboiled and then dried. Others are made more porous than traditional lasagna noodles. Precooked lasagna noodles are designed to absorb liquid from the other ingredients in the dish while they bake, resulting in wonderfully flavored al dente noodles in no time. It's best not to substitute regular noodles for precooked noodles.

2 teaspoons olive oil
5 cups finely chopped mushrooms (about 1 pound)
1½ cups chopped onion
2 tablespoons chopped fresh thyme
2 garlic cloves, minced
¼ cup dry white wine
2 (6.5-ounce) cans lump crabmeat
1 pound uncooked large shrimp
2 cups water
1½ teaspoons celery salt
1 teaspoon fennel seeds
1¼ cups (5 ounces) crumbled goat or feta cheese
1 cup 2% reduced-fat cottage cheese
¼ cup finely chopped fresh basil
1 tablespoon fresh lemon juice
1 garlic clove, minced
¼ cup all-purpose flour
1 cup 1% low-fat milk
¼ cup (1 ounce) grated fresh Parmesan cheese
Cooking spray
1 (8-ounce) package precooked lasagna noodles
2 cups (8 ounces) shredded part-skim mozzarella cheese
¼ cup chopped fresh flat-leaf parsley

1. Heat oil in a large nonstick skillet over medium heat. Add mushrooms, onion, thyme, and 2 garlic cloves; cook 10 minutes, stirring occasionally. Add wine. Bring to a boil; cook 1½ minutes or until liquid almost evaporates. Remove from heat; stir in crabmeat. Set aside.
2. Peel and devein shrimp, reserving shells. Cut each shrimp in half lengthwise; cover and refrigerate. Combine reserved shrimp shells, 2 cups water, celery salt, and fennel seeds in a small saucepan. Bring to a boil; cook until reduced to 1½ cups shrimp stock (about 15 minutes). Strain stock through a sieve into a bowl; discard solids. Set stock aside.
3. Combine goat cheese, cottage cheese, basil, lemon juice, and 1 garlic clove; set aside.
4. Preheat oven to 375°.
5. Lightly spoon flour into a dry measuring cup, and level with a knife. Place flour in a small saucepan; gradually add milk, stirring with a whisk. Stir in shrimp stock; bring to a boil. Reduce heat; simmer 5 minutes or until thick, stirring constantly. Remove from heat; stir in Parmesan cheese.
6. Spread ½ cup sauce in bottom of a 13 x 9–inch baking dish coated with cooking spray. Arrange 4 noodles, slightly overlapping, over sauce; top with one-third goat cheese mixture, one-third crab mixture, one-third shrimp, ⅔ cup sauce, and ⅔ cup mozzarella. Repeat layers twice, ending with mozzarella. Bake at 375° for 40 minutes or until golden. Let stand 15 minutes. Sprinkle with parsley. Yield: 8 servings.

CALORIES 428 (29% from fat); FAT 13.9g (sat 7.7g, mono 2.5g, poly 1.1g); PROTEIN 40.1g; CARB 33.6g; FIBER 3.6g; CHOL 143mg; IRON 4.1mg; SODIUM 934mg; CALC 414mg

You can always splurge on fresh crabmeat, but we found that canned lump crabmeat works just as well in this recipe. Shrimp shells render a quick stock to flavor the sauce. To save prep time, we used precooked lasagna noodles.

Sage Risotto with Fresh Mozzarella and Prosciutto

Fresh mozzarella is so luxurious, with its subtle, rich flavor and texture. It comes shaped like a ball or large egg, and is stored in brine to keep it fresh. The round shape and texture make it difficult to shred. It's easier to cut the cheese into rounds and finely chop. Finely chopped mozzarella melts but doesn't completely disperse in this risotto, leaving little pockets of warm cheese to surprise and please you.

2 (14-ounce) cans fat-free, less-sodium chicken broth
1 tablespoon butter
1 cup finely chopped leek (about 2 small leeks)
2 garlic cloves, minced
1¼ cups Arborio rice
¼ teaspoon salt
½ cup dry white wine
1½ to 2 tablespoons finely chopped fresh sage
1 cup (4 ounces) finely chopped fresh mozzarella cheese
2 ounces prosciutto, chopped (about ⅓ cup)
¼ teaspoon freshly ground black pepper
Sage sprigs (optional)

1. Bring broth to a simmer (do not boil). Keep warm over low heat.

2. Melt butter in a medium sauté pan over medium heat. Add leek and garlic, and cook 3 minutes, stirring frequently. Add rice and salt; cook 1 minute, stirring constantly. Stir in wine; cook 2 minutes or until liquid is nearly absorbed, stirring constantly. Add broth, ½ cup at a time, stirring frequently until each portion is absorbed before adding the next (about 20 minutes total). Stir in chopped sage, and cook 2 minutes. Remove from heat; stir in mozzarella. Spoon 1 cup risotto into each of 4 bowls; top each serving with about 1½ tablespoons prosciutto. Sprinkle with black pepper. Garnish with sage sprigs, if desired. Yield: 4 servings.

CALORIES 443 (25% from fat); FAT 12.3g (sat 7g, mono 3g, poly 1g); PROTEIN 18.8g; CARB 59.6g; FIBER 1.4g; CHOL 43mg; IRON 1.3mg; SODIUM 863mg; CALC 193mg

Ever since northern Italians first stirred Arborio rice into a gooey risotto, cooks there have cast any remotely creamy grain-based dish as a risotto. This dish sticks more closely to the original than some more recent versions. You may substitute basil for sage, if desired.

Beet Risotto with Greens, Goat Cheese, and Walnuts

Fresh beets have become as common on fine-restaurant menus as they once were in sensible root cellars. With hues ranging from yellow to purple, they lend themselves to dramatic presentations. You may use a combo of golden and red beets in the risotto recipe, but keep in mind that the red-colored beets will be the stars. When preparing beets for cooking, peel them, as they have tough skins like most other root vegetables. Peeling a beet is like peeling an apple, except for the stains that beets may leave with you. To avoid stains, hold the beet with a gloved hand, and peel away its skin with a vegetable peeler.

2 teaspoons olive oil
1 cup chopped onion
1 cup Arborio rice
1 tablespoon minced peeled fresh ginger
2 teaspoons finely chopped fresh rosemary
½ cup dry white wine
3 cups finely chopped peeled beets (about 1 pound)
½ cup water
¼ teaspoon fine sea salt
1 (14½-ounce) can vegetable broth
6 cups finely sliced Swiss chard
½ cup (2 ounces) crumbled goat cheese
¼ cup chopped walnuts, toasted
Rosemary sprigs (optional)

1. Heat oil in a Dutch oven over medium-high heat. Add onion; sauté 3 minutes. Add rice, ginger, and rosemary; sauté 1 minute. Add wine; cook 3 minutes or until liquid is nearly absorbed, stirring constantly.

2. Add beets, water, salt, and broth; bring to a boil. Cover, reduce heat, and simmer 20 minutes or until beets are tender, stirring occasionally.

3. Stir in chard; cook 5 minutes. Add cheese, stirring until blended. Sprinkle with walnuts. Garnish with rosemary sprigs, if desired. Yield: 4 servings (serving size: 1½ cups and 1 tablespoon walnuts).

CALORIES 412 (30% from fat); FAT 13.7g (sat 4.9g, mono 4g, poly 3.6g); PROTEIN 14.1g; CARB 57.5g; FIBER 4.1g; CHOL 14mg; IRON 2.1mg; SODIUM 611mg; CALC 92mg

Stunning appearance. Satisfying textures. Great flavor. These are just some of this risotto's amazing attributes. The earthiness of the beets and Swiss chard mixed with creamy goat cheese and crunchy walnuts truly make this a one-dish meatless-main wonder. And, unlike a traditional risotto, it's not so labor intensive since it doesn't have to be stirred constantly. Before you sauté the onion, we suggest that you toast the walnuts in the Dutch oven. They will add a nice fragrance.

Creamy Two-Cheese Polenta

4 cups 1% low-fat milk
1 cup water
1¼ teaspoons salt
¼ teaspoon freshly ground black pepper
1¼ cups instant dry polenta
⅓ cup (about 2½ ounces) mascarpone cheese
⅓ cup (about 1½ ounces) grated Parmigiano-Reggiano cheese
Freshly ground pepper (optional)

1. Combine first 4 ingredients in a medium saucepan over medium-high heat. Bring to a boil; gradually add polenta, stirring constantly with a whisk. Cook 2 minutes or until thick, stirring constantly. Remove from heat; stir in cheeses. Serve immediately. Yield: 8 servings (serving size: about ⅔ cup).

CALORIES 206 (28% from fat); FAT 6.4g (sat 3.7g, mono 0.7g, poly 0.1g); PROTEIN 8.5g; CARB 28.7g; FIBER 2.5g; CHOL 19mg; IRON 0.6mg; SODIUM 493mg; CALC 207mg

Mascarpone is a sweet, delicate, triple-blended cheese made from cow's milk. Originally from Italy's Lombardy region, the cheese is quite versatile and is an Italian favorite when served with fresh fruit. Here it's paired with Parmigiano-Reggiano, a dry, hard cheese, resulting in a flavorful combination that enhances both the taste and texture of this dish. While some cooks believe that cream cheese is a suitable substitution for mascarpone, our Test Kitchens prefer Fromage blanc or Quark (yogurt cheese). These cheeses are also fresh cheeses that are neither aged or ripened.

This mildly flavored staff favorite pairs nicely with a spicy main dish such as Herb, Garlic, and Mustard-Crusted Fillet of Beef on page 90. The polenta is best served immediately, but if you have to wait a few minutes, keep it warm by covering it and placing it over very low heat. Stir occasionally.

Polenta with Roasted Red Peppers and Fontina Cheese

3 large red bell peppers
1 (14.5-ounce) can whole
   tomatoes, undrained and
   chopped
Cooking spray
1 (16-ounce) tube of polenta,
   cut crosswise into 12 slices
1¼ cups (5 ounces) shredded
   fontina cheese
Fresh basil (optional)

Polenta is an Italian dish made by cooking cornmeal with liquid until it forms a soft mush. As a shortcut to making polenta in a saucepan, this recipe calls for precooked polenta. Look for plain and flavored 16-ounce tubes of polenta in the produce section of your supermarket. This precooked polenta works well in recipes in which it is cut into slices or cubes and sautéed, baked, or grilled. To slice the polenta crosswise, place it horizontally on a cutting board, and slice through its width for the desired amount of slices.

1. Preheat broiler.
2. Cut peppers in half lengthwise; discard seeds and membranes. Place pepper halves, skin sides up, on a foil-lined baking sheet; flatten with hand. Broil 10 minutes or until blackened. Place in a zip-top plastic bag; seal. Let stand 15 minutes. Peel and cut into strips.
3. Preheat oven to 350°.
4. Drain tomatoes in a sieve over a bowl; reserve liquid. Heat a large skillet over medium-low heat; add tomatoes. Cook 1 minute. Gradually add tomato liquid; simmer 1 minute. Add pepper strips, and simmer 5 minutes. Remove mixture from heat.
5. Spread ¼ cup pepper sauce in bottom of a 13 x 9–inch baking dish coated with cooking spray. Arrange polenta slices over pepper sauce, and spread remaining pepper sauce over polenta. Sprinkle with fontina cheese. Bake at 350° for 25 minutes. Garnish with fresh basil, if desired. Yield: 6 servings.

CALORIES 187 (38% from fat); FAT 7.8g (sat 4.6g, mono 2.1g, poly 0.6g); PROTEIN 9.2g; CARB 20.2g; FIBER 3.4g; CHOL 27mg; IRON 2.4mg; SODIUM 622mg; CALC 151mg

This meatless main dish features just four ingredients: red bell peppers, tomatoes, polenta, and fontina cheese. Although it uses convenience items like prepared polenta and canned tomatoes, it does so in a food-savvy way by providing speed without sacrificing quality. Hands-on preparation time is less than 15 minutes.

entrées

Grouper with Puttanesca Sauce

A grill pan adds more than just pretty grill marks and smoky flavors. Its ridges elevate food so air can circulate underneath and fat can drip away. Your food doesn't sauté or steam as it does in a plain skillet; instead, flavor is seared into it. Meat and fish turn out juicy, with no need for added fat. Vegetables stay crisp-tender, and their nutrients don't leach out into the cooking water. You can buy a grill pan at your local discount or kitchen store for less than $20 to more than $100.

Cooking spray
4 (6-ounce) grouper or flounder fillets
⅛ teaspoon salt
¼ teaspoon black pepper
1½ teaspoons olive oil
1 cup thinly sliced onion
1 tablespoon bottled minced garlic
¼ teaspoon dried oregano
1 (28-ounce) can whole tomatoes, drained
⅓ cup chopped pitted kalamata olives
2 tablespoons capers
¼ cup chopped fresh flat-leaf parsley (optional)

1. Heat a nonstick grill pan over medium-high heat. Coat pan with cooking spray. Sprinkle fish with salt and pepper. Add fish to pan; cook 5 minutes on each side or until fish flakes easily when tested with a fork.
2. While fish cooks, heat oil in a large nonstick skillet over medium heat. Add onion; cook 4 minutes or until tender, stirring frequently. Add garlic, oregano, and tomatoes; bring to a boil. Reduce heat, and simmer 6 minutes, stirring frequently. Stir in olives and capers; cook 1 minute. Spoon tomato mixture over fish. Sprinkle with chopped parsley, if desired. Yield: 4 servings (serving size: 1 fillet and ¾ cup tomato mixture).

CALORIES 238 (18% from fat); FAT 4.8g (sat 0.8g, mono 2.5g, poly 0.8g); PROTEIN 35.5g; CARB 12g; FIBER 1.5g; CHOL 63mg; IRON 2.4mg; SODIUM 736mg; CALC 142mg

Take your taste buds to Italy! The robust, spicy sauce is a chunky mixture of tomatoes, onions, capers, olives, and garlic. The word puttanesca *(poot-tah-NEHS-kah) comes from* puttana, *for ladies of the night. Legend has it that the ladies lured men to their houses with this intensely fragrant sauce. It's most often served over pasta, but it tastes terrific spooned over filet mignon, chicken, or fish, or tossed with shrimp. Keep your pantry stocked with the sauce ingredients to make this dish anytime. The prep time is kept to a minimum by capitalizing on high-flavor ingredients. Serve with orzo to soak up the sauce, and enjoy your culinary journey.*

Broiled Red Snapper with Sicilian Tomato Pesto

Red snapper, the most prized member of the large snapper family, has a sweet flavor, similar to shrimp. It's a versatile fish, making it a good choice for recipes that call for baking, broiling, pan-frying, or grilling. To test the fish for doneness, flake it with a fork while it's on the broiler pan. It should flake easily, but have more resistance and be firmer than delicate fish such as flounder, sole, cod, or orange roughy.

Pesto:
2 cups basil leaves
2 tablespoons pine nuts, toasted
2 tablespoons extravirgin olive oil
2 garlic cloves, minced
¼ cup (1 ounce) grated Parmigiano-Reggiano cheese
⅛ teaspoon crushed red pepper
1½ cups chopped plum tomato (about 3 medium)
½ teaspoon salt
½ teaspoon freshly ground black pepper

Fish:
6 (6-ounce) red snapper or other firm whitefish fillets
¼ teaspoon salt
Cooking spray

Remaining Ingredient:
3 cups hot cooked orzo

1. To prepare pesto, place first 4 ingredients in a food processor; process until smooth. Add cheese and red pepper; process until blended. Transfer mixture to a bowl. Add tomato, ½ teaspoon salt, and black pepper, stirring gently to combine.

2. Preheat broiler.

3. To prepare fish, sprinkle fish with ¼ teaspoon salt. Arrange fish on a broiler pan coated with cooking spray, and broil 8 minutes or until fish flakes easily when tested with a fork. Place orzo on each of 6 plates, and top each serving with fish and pesto. Yield: 6 servings (serving size: ½ cup orzo, 1 fillet, and ¼ cup pesto).

CALORIES 437 (22% from fat); FAT 10.8g (sat 2.4, mono 4.8, poly 2); PROTEIN 44.9g; CARB 38.9g; FIBER 3.1g; CHOL 67mg; IRON 2.9mg; SODIUM 497mg; CALC 156mg

In-season tomatoes enliven almost any meal. Plum tomatoes, also called Roma or Italian tomatoes, work best in this recipe because they have a low water content and few seeds; juicier tomatoes would thin the pesto. No need to seed or peel them. You can make the pesto ahead and keep it chilled. Stir in the tomatoes just before serving.

Sautéed Scallops with Parsley and Garlic

16 large sea scallops (about
   1½ pounds)
¼ teaspoon salt
¼ teaspoon freshly ground
   black pepper
1½ tablespoons olive oil,
   divided
2 tablespoons butter
¼ cup chopped fresh flat-leaf
   parsley
2 garlic cloves, minced

1. Sprinkle scallops with salt and pepper. Heat 2¼ teaspoons oil in a large nonstick skillet over medium-high heat. Add 8 scallops; sauté 2½ minutes on each side or until browned. Set aside, and keep warm. Repeat procedure with remaining 2¼ teaspoons oil and 8 scallops. Wipe pan clean with a paper towel.
2. Add butter to pan; reduce heat, and cook until butter melts. Stir in parsley and garlic, and cook 15 seconds. Return scallops to pan; toss to coat. Yield: 4 servings (serving size: 4 scallops).

CALORIES 241 (43% from fat); FAT 11.5g (sat 3.6g, mono 5.7g, poly 1.1g); PROTEIN 28.7g; CARB 4.3g; FIBER 0.2g; CHOL 71mg; IRON 0.8mg; SODIUM 464mg; CALC 48mg

The secret to perfectly browned scallops is patience; we recommend cooking them in batches. Begin by patting the scallops with paper towels to remove excess moisture. Heat the oil until it ripples in the pan. Add the scallops, a few at a time, and wait for them to sizzle before adding more. If you add too many at once, the pan will lose heat, the scallops will take longer to brown, and they may overcook, resulting in tough, dry scallops.

Because Italy is a peninsula, seafood is abundant and is a staple in Italian cuisine. As with their produce, Italians demand freshness for seafood, particularly scallops. Sea scallops are almost always shucked at sea. Look for scallops that are labeled "dry" or "unsoaked" and that are cream-colored or slightly pink. Avoid those that are pure white, brownish, dull looking, or are labeled "wet." These scallops have been soaked in a solution which causes them to absorb water and lose flavor. Ask to smell the scallops; they shouldn't have a strong odor.

Shrimp Scampi

2 teaspoons olive oil
28 large shrimp, peeled and
   deveined (about 1½ pounds)
3 garlic cloves, minced
⅓ cup sauvignon blanc or
   other dry white wine
½ teaspoon salt
¼ teaspoon freshly ground
   black pepper
¼ cup chopped fresh flat-leaf
   parsley
1 tablespoon fresh lemon juice

1. Heat oil in a large skillet over medium-high heat. Add shrimp; sauté 1 minute. Add garlic; sauté 1 minute. Stir in wine, salt, and pepper; bring mixture to a boil. Reduce heat to medium; cook 30 seconds. Add parsley and juice; toss well to coat. Cook 1 minute or until shrimp are done. Yield: 4 servings (serving size: about 7 shrimp).

CALORIES 220 (21% from fat); FAT 5.2g (sat 0.9g, mono 2.1g, poly 1.3g); PROTEIN 34.9g; CARB 3.1g; FIBER 0.2g; CHOL 259mg; IRON 4.5mg; SODIUM 546mg; CALC 100mg

We use shrimp in many of our recipes because of its unique flavor, versatility, and largely year-round availability. Sometimes we recommend that the shrimp be deveined. However, except for the largest shrimp, there's neither danger nor distaste in leaving the thin black line—the vein—right where it is. Since we call for large deveined shrimp in Shrimp Scampi, you may want to devein them yourself. It's actually quite simple. Here's how: Using a small knife or shrimp deveiner, make a slit down the back of the shrimp, and remove the vein.

Scampi is a Venetian dialect word for a local prawn that you won't find very often in American markets. As a substitute, American cooks use shrimp and cook it with lots of garlic. Serve with a piece of crusty Italian bread to sop up the tangy, garlic-rich sauce.

Herb, Garlic, and Mustard-Crusted Fillet of Beef

Always use a meat thermometer to guarantee that meats are cooked to the right temperature. There are two types of meat thermometers: probe-type and instant-read. We prefer to use the probe-type for large cuts of meat such as the beef tenderloin in this recipe. Insert the thermometer into the meat (not touching fat or bone) before putting it into the oven. Leave it in the meat until the proper temperature is reached. Beef should be cooked to 145° for medium-rare, 160° for medium, and 170° for well done.

1 (2-pound) beef tenderloin, trimmed
Cooking spray
¾ teaspoon salt
¼ teaspoon freshly ground black pepper
3 tablespoons Dijon mustard
¼ cup chopped fresh basil
¼ cup chopped fresh parsley
1 tablespoon chopped fresh thyme
1 tablespoon chopped fresh oregano
3 garlic cloves, minced

1. Preheat oven to 400°.
2. Place beef on a broiler pan coated with cooking spray; sprinkle with salt and pepper. Spread mustard evenly over beef. Combine remaining ingredients; pat evenly over beef.
3. Insert a meat thermometer into thickest portion of beef. Bake at 400° for 40 minutes or until thermometer registers 145° (medium-rare) or desired degree of doneness.
4. Transfer beef to a cutting board. Cover loosely with foil, and let stand 10 minutes before slicing. Yield: 8 servings (serving size: 3 ounces).

CALORIES 154 (43% from fat); FAT 7.4g (sat 2.6g, mono 2.8g, poly 0.4g); PROTEIN 19.8g; CARB 1.4g; FIBER 0.3g; CHOL 57mg; IRON 2.8mg; SODIUM 404mg; CALC 23mg

For a change of pace, give an Italian-inspired menu a try at your next holiday gathering. With the fillet of beef as the main attraction, complete the meal with a green salad, Creamy Two-Cheese Polenta (recipe on page 76), sautéed leeks and broccolini, Ciabatta (recipe on page 104), and a decadent slice of Chocolate-Walnut Cake (recipe on page 132). To make a sauce for the beef, deglaze the pan with red wine, and reduce it. Be sure to use a dry, well-structured, powerful red that can stand up to the beef, such as a cabernet sauvignon.

Osso Buco with Gremolata

The small, silvery colored anchovy is found in the Mediterranean Sea and off the coast of southern Europe. These fish are commonly filleted, salt-cured, and then canned in oil. Most often used to flavor sauces, dressings, or appetizers, their salty taste can be overpowering if used in excess. One anchovy fillet is the equivalent to ½ teaspoon anchovy paste. The paste is formed from pounded anchovies mixed with vinegar and spices. Anchovy paste is normally sold in a tube and can be found in your local supermarket. Leftover anchovy paste may be refrigerated for up to one month.

Osso Buco:
  ⅔ cup all-purpose flour
  ¾ teaspoon freshly ground black pepper, divided
  ½ teaspoon kosher salt, divided
  6 veal shanks, trimmed (about 5 pounds)
  2 teaspoons butter, divided
  2 teaspoons olive oil, divided
  2 cups coarsely chopped red onion
1½ cups chopped celery
  6 garlic cloves, minced
  4 cups beef broth
  2 cups dry white wine
  1 tablespoon chopped fresh rosemary
  1 tablespoon anchovy paste

Gremolata:
  ½ cup chopped fresh flat-leaf parsley
  1 tablespoon grated lemon rind
  2 garlic cloves, minced

Remaining Ingredient:
  8 cups hot cooked pappardelle (wide ribbon pasta; about 1 pound uncooked pasta)

1. To prepare osso buco, combine flour, ¼ teaspoon pepper, and ¼ teaspoon salt in a shallow dish. Dredge veal in flour mixture.

2. Heat 1 teaspoon butter and 1 teaspoon oil in a large skillet over medium heat. Add half of veal; cook 6 minutes, browning on both sides. Place browned veal in a 7-quart electric slow cooker. Repeat procedure with 1 teaspoon butter, 1 teaspoon oil, and remaining veal.

3. Add onion and celery to pan; sauté over medium-high heat 5 minutes or until tender. Add 6 garlic cloves to pan; sauté 1 minute. Stir in broth, wine, rosemary, and anchovy paste, scraping pan to loosen browned bits. Bring to a boil; cook 4 minutes. Pour over veal.

4. Cover and cook on LOW 9 hours or until done. Sprinkle veal with ½ teaspoon pepper and ¼ teaspoon salt. Remove veal from cooker; cool slightly. Remove veal from bones, and cut up.

5. To prepare gremolata, combine parsley, lemon rind, and 2 garlic cloves. Place pasta in each of 8 pasta bowls. Top each serving with veal and broth mixture. Reserve remaining broth mixture for another use. Sprinkle each serving with gremolata. Yield: 8 servings (serving size: 1 cup pasta, ⅔ cup veal, ½ cup broth mixture, and 1 tablespoon gremolata).

CALORIES 443 (25% from fat); FAT 12.2g (sat 4.1g, mono 4.9g, poly 1.1g); PROTEIN 54.9g; CARB 15.9g; FIBER 1.8g; CHOL 200mg; IRON 3.3mg; SODIUM 485mg; CALC 94mg

Veal shanks, called ossobuco *in Italian, or "bone with a hole," are inexpensive and become a succulent meal in the slow cooker. Even if you aren't an anchovy lover, don't omit the anchovy paste—it adds immeasurably to the flavor. Use the remaining broth mixture in soups and stews.*

Lamb Shanks
on Cannellini Beans

Odori is the Italian version of the French *mirepoix*—a colorful, fine mix of aromatics including onion, carrot, celery, and garlic that provides a rich flavor base to sauces, soups, and entrées. To chop the vegetables, use one hand to grip the handle of a chef's knife, and place the other hand on the blunt edge of the knife. Keep the knife tip on the cutting surface while rapidly lifting the handle up and down, cutting through the food. Continue chopping until the pieces are the desired size: coarsely chopped, chopped, or in this instance, finely chopped.

6 (¾-pound) lamb shanks, trimmed
½ teaspoon salt
¼ teaspoon black pepper
2 cups finely chopped carrot
1 cup finely chopped onion
1 cup finely chopped celery
1 cup dry red wine
½ cup beef broth
1½ teaspoons dried rosemary
2 (14.5-ounce) cans diced tomatoes
2 bay leaves
1 cup dried cannellini beans or other white beans
4 bacon slices
4 garlic cloves, sliced
Rosemary sprigs (optional)

1. Sprinkle lamb with salt and pepper. Heat a large non-stick skillet over medium-high heat. Add lamb; cook 12 minutes, browning on all sides. Remove from pan. Add carrot, onion, and celery; sauté 3 minutes. Add wine. Bring to a boil; cook 5 minutes. Stir in broth, dried rosemary, tomatoes, and bay leaves. Return lamb to pan (pan will be very full). Cover, reduce heat, and simmer 2 hours or until lamb is very tender, turning lamb once. Remove lamb from pan; bring liquid to a boil, and cook 5 minutes. Discard bay leaves.

2. While lamb cooks, sort and wash beans; place in a large Dutch oven. Cover with water to 2 inches above beans; bring to a boil, and cook 2 minutes. Remove from heat; cover and let stand 1 hour. Drain beans; place in Dutch oven. Cover with water to 2 inches above beans, and bring to a boil. Reduce heat, and simmer 1 hour or until tender. Drain.

3. Cook bacon in Dutch oven over medium-high heat until crisp. Remove bacon from pan, reserving 2 teaspoons drippings. Crumble bacon. Heat drippings over medium-high heat. Add garlic; sauté 2 minutes or until golden. Stir in beans and bacon; remove from heat.

4. Place beans on each of 6 plates; arrange lamb on beans. Spoon sauce over lamb. Garnish with rosemary sprigs, if desired. Yield: 6 servings (serving size: ⅔ cup beans, 1 shank, and 1⅓ cups sauce).

CALORIES 506 (26% from fat); FAT 14.5g (sat 5.1g, mono 5.9g, poly 1.7g); PROTEIN 60.2g; CARB 32.9g; FIBER 6.3g; CHOL 156mg; IRON 8.3mg; SODIUM 791mg; CALC 130mg

Cooking the beans and lamb at the same time frees you to work on other recipes. We loved the dried beans, but for a quicker approach, substitute drained canned beans. Just stir them in along with the bacon.

Pork Saltimbocca with Polenta

Folding and stuffing meat is an easy way to perk up your favorite meals. To flatten the pork for this recipe, sandwich the meat between two sheets of plastic wrap. With a rolling pin or the flat side of a meat mallet, strike the meat in the center at its thickest part, moving outward as you continue. Once you have reached the desired thickness, spread the filling on the meat. Fold the chop in half, trapping the filling inside, and secure with a toothpick to hold it together. The resulting dish is a tender, tasty pork chop with a cheesy surprise inside.

Pork:

- 6 (4-ounce) boneless center-cut loin pork chops, trimmed
- 6 very thin slices prosciutto (about 2 ounces)
- 6 large sage leaves
- 1/3 cup (about 1 1/2 ounces) shredded fontina cheese
- 1/4 teaspoon freshly ground black pepper
- 1/8 teaspoon salt
- 2 tablespoons all-purpose flour
- 1 tablespoon olive oil
- 1/2 cup dry white wine
- 1 cup fat-free, less-sodium chicken broth
- 1 tablespoon thinly sliced fresh sage

Polenta:

- 2 cups 2% reduced-fat milk
- 1 (14-ounce) can fat-free, less-sodium chicken broth
- 1 cup instant polenta
- 1/2 teaspoon salt

1. To prepare pork, place each chop between 2 sheets of heavy-duty plastic wrap; pound to 1/4-inch thickness using a meat mallet or rolling pin. Arrange 1 prosciutto slice over each chop; top with 1 sage leaf and about 1 tablespoon cheese. Fold chops in half to sandwich filling, and secure with wooden picks. Sprinkle both sides of chops with pepper and 1/8 teaspoon salt. Place flour in a shallow dish; dredge stuffed chops in flour.

2. Heat oil in a large nonstick skillet over medium-high heat. Add chops, and cook 3 minutes on each side or until done. Remove chops from pan; cover and keep warm.

3. Add wine to pan, scraping pan to loosen browned bits; cook until reduced to 1/4 cup (about 2 minutes). Add 1 cup broth, and bring to a boil. Cook until reduced to 1/2 cup (about 5 minutes). Stir in 1 tablespoon sage. Reduce heat to medium. Return chops to pan; cook 2 minutes or until thoroughly heated, turning once.

4. To prepare polenta, combine milk and 1 can broth in a medium saucepan; bring to a boil. Gradually stir in polenta and 1/2 teaspoon salt. Cover, reduce heat to medium-low, and cook 2 minutes. Serve polenta immediately with pork chops and sauce. Yield: 6 servings (serving size: 1/2 cup polenta, 1 stuffed chop, and about 4 teaspoons sauce).

CALORIES 404 (30% from fat); FAT 13.3g (sat 5.3g, mono 6g, poly 1g); PROTEIN 34.9g; CARB 30.8g; FIBER 2.8g; CHOL 85mg; IRON 1.6mg; SODIUM 733mg; CALC 172mg

Traditional saltimbocca is made with thin slices of pounded veal, but lean pork chops update this recipe and provide more flavor. The buttery overtones of fontina cheese are also a pleasant addition. Top with a whole sage leaf for a handsome presentation.

Herbed Chicken Parmesan

By using a commercial pasta sauce in this recipe, you can save yourself preparation time. Though any of your favorite tomato-basil sauces will do, we recommend using an organic sauce. Organic tomatoes and basil blend together to form a natural-tasting, fat-free sauce that's simply superior.

1⅓ cups (1½ ounces) shredded fresh Parmesan cheese, divided
¼ cup dry breadcrumbs
1 tablespoon minced fresh flat-leaf parsley
½ teaspoon dried basil
¼ teaspoon salt, divided
1 large egg white, lightly beaten
1 pound chicken breast tenders
1 tablespoon butter
1½ cups bottled fat-free tomato-basil pasta sauce
2 teaspoons balsamic vinegar
¼ teaspoon black pepper
⅓ cup (1½ ounces) shredded provolone cheese

1. Preheat broiler.
2. Combine 2 tablespoons Parmesan, breadcrumbs, parsley, basil, and ⅛ teaspoon salt in a shallow dish. Place egg white in a shallow dish. Dip each chicken tender in egg white; dredge in breadcrumb mixture. Melt butter in a large nonstick skillet over medium-high heat. Add chicken; cook 3 minutes on each side or until done. Set aside.
3. Combine ⅛ teaspoon salt, pasta sauce, vinegar, and pepper in a microwave-safe bowl. Cover with plastic wrap; vent. Microwave mixture at HIGH 2 minutes or until thoroughly heated. Pour sauce over chicken in pan. Sprinkle evenly with remaining Parmesan and provolone cheese. Wrap handle of pan with foil; broil 2 minutes or until cheese melts. Yield: 4 servings.

CALORIES 308 (30% from fat); FAT 10.4g (sat 5.7g, mono 3g, poly 0.6g); PROTEIN 35.9g; CARB 16.2g; FIBER 1.8g; CHOL 88mg; IRON 2.3mg; SODIUM 808mg; CALC 249mg

Dredging ordinary chicken breast tenders in a breadcrumb mixture transforms them into a golden-brown, tried-and-true dinner delight. Topped with ruby red tomato-basil pasta sauce and smothered in iconic Parmesan and provolone cheeses, they'll become a staple at your family table. We recommend serving rice-shaped orzo pasta with this saucy entrée, but you can use spaghetti or angel hair pasta instead. Round out the menu with roasted lemon-garlic broccoli—and don't forget the wine.

(pictured on cover)

Chicken Cacciatore

Also known as *boletes, cèpes,* or *steinpilze,* porcini mushrooms are most often found dried in the United States. You can sometimes find them fresh at specialty markets during the late spring and early fall. If you find fresh porcinis, choose those that are pale to tan in color and avoid those that crumble easily. Porcini lend a smooth texture and earthy flavor to meals. They're especially popular in soups and stews, or, as they're used here, as the base for a flavorful sauce.

1 (½-ounce) package dried porcini mushrooms
1 cup boiling water
2 teaspoons olive oil
8 skinless, boneless chicken thighs (about 1 pound)
1 teaspoon salt
½ teaspoon freshly ground black pepper
3 garlic cloves, minced
3 tablespoons minced fresh parsley, divided
¾ cup canned crushed tomatoes
½ cup fat-free, less-sodium chicken broth
½ cup water

1. Combine mushrooms and boiling water in a bowl; cover and let stand 30 minutes. Remove mushrooms with a slotted spoon. Finely chop mushrooms; set aside. Strain soaking liquid into a bowl through a sieve lined with cheesecloth or paper towels. Discard solids; reserve soaking liquid.

2. Heat oil in a large nonstick skillet over medium-high heat. Sprinkle chicken with salt and pepper. Add chicken to pan; cook 4 minutes on each side or until browned. Remove chicken from pan. Reduce heat to medium. Add garlic to pan; sauté 2 minutes or until golden, stirring constantly. Add 2 tablespoons parsley; cook 30 seconds. Add chopped mushrooms; cook 30 seconds. Stir in reserved soaking liquid, tomatoes, broth, and water; bring to a simmer. Return chicken to pan, and reduce heat to low. Cover and cook 10 minutes or until chicken is done.

3. Remove chicken; keep warm. Increase heat to medium-high; cook until sauce is reduced to 1 cup (about 5 minutes). Spoon sauce over chicken; sprinkle with 1 tablespoon parsley. Yield: 4 servings (serving size: 2 chicken thighs and ¼ cup sauce).

CALORIES 263 (29% from fat); FAT 8.5g (sat 1.7g, mono 3.7g, poly 1.8g); PROTEIN 33.6g; CARB 11.7g; FIBER 3.5g; CHOL 115mg; IRON 5.7mg; SODIUM 771mg; CALC 32mg

Cacciatore (kah-chuh-TOR-ee) refers to an Italian dish that's prepared in the "hunter's style." Differing legends revolve around this dish—some say the dish was cooked for the hunter as a send-off before a hunt; others recount that the dish was created with the hunting bounty. Regardless, this dish is the ultimate Italian comfort food. Serve it with a glass of Chianti, a classic Italian red wine made principally from Sangiovese grapes.

bread, panini & pizza

Ciabatta

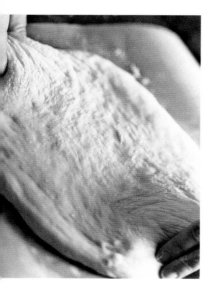

The slipper-like shape of ciabatta is so easy to achieve. With each oval of dough, simply taper the ends with your fingers to form a slipper shape. Let the dough rise in a warm place (85°), free from drafts, 45 minutes or until doubled in size. Then you're ready to bake.

Sponge:
- 1 cup bread flour
- ½ cup warm fat-free milk (100° to 110°)
- ¼ cup warm water (100° to 110°)
- 1 tablespoon honey
- 1 package dry yeast (about 2¼ teaspoons)

Dough:
- 3½ cups bread flour, divided
- ½ cup semolina or pasta flour
- ¾ cup warm water (100° to 110°)
- ½ cup warm fat-free milk (100° to 110°)
- 1½ teaspoons salt
- 1 package dry yeast (about 2¼ teaspoons)
- 3 tablespoons semolina or pasta flour, divided

1. To prepare sponge, lightly spoon 1 cup flour into a dry measuring cup; level with a knife. Combine 1 cup flour, milk, and next 3 ingredients in a large bowl, stirring well with a whisk. Cover; chill 12 hours.

2. To prepare dough, let sponge stand at room temperature 30 minutes. Lightly spoon 3½ cups bread flour and ½ cup semolina flour into dry measuring cups, and level with a knife. Add 3 cups bread flour, ½ cup semolina flour, ¾ cup warm water, ½ cup warm milk, salt, and 1 package yeast to sponge; stir well to form a soft dough. Turn dough out onto a floured surface. Knead until smooth and elastic (about 8 minutes), and add enough of remaining bread flour, 1 tablespoon at a time, to prevent dough from sticking to hands. Divide dough in half.

3. Working with one portion at a time (cover remaining dough to prevent drying), roll into a 13 x 5–inch oval. Place, 3 inches apart, on a large baking sheet sprinkled with 2 tablespoons semolina flour. Taper ends of dough to form a "slipper." Sprinkle 1 tablespoon semolina flour over dough. Cover and let rise in a warm place (85°), free from drafts, 45 minutes or until doubled in size.

4. Preheat oven to 425°.

5. Uncover dough. Bake at 425° for 18 minutes or until loaves are lightly browned and sound hollow when tapped. Remove from pan, and cool on a wire rack. Yield: 2 loaves, 16 servings (serving size: 1 slice).

CALORIES 150 (1% from fat); FAT 0.1g (sat 0g, mono 0.1g, poly 0g); PROTEIN 6.3g; CARB 32.1g; FIBER 1.3g; CHOL 0mg; IRON 2.1mg; SODIUM 227mg; CALC 21mg

Make your own European bread at home for only a fraction of what it would cost at a local bakery. Ciabatta (chyah-BAH-tah), a rustic yeast bread which originated in Italy, gets its name from its unique shape—translated, ciabatta means "slipper." You can get a really nice crust if you use a pizza stone, but a baking sheet works fine, too.

Olive and Asiago Rolls

Cutting or slashing the dough after the second rise allows it to expand during baking. Use scissors or a very sharp knife to cut a ¼-inch-deep "X" in the top of each roll.

1 tablespoon sugar
1 package dry yeast (about 2¼ teaspoons)
¾ cup warm water (100° to 110°)
3⅔ cups bread flour
½ cup whole wheat flour
¾ cup 1% low-fat milk
2 tablespoons chopped fresh oregano
1 teaspoon salt
1 teaspoon olive oil
Cooking spray
3 tablespoons chopped pitted kalamata olives
1 tablespoon water
1 large egg white, lightly beaten
½ cup (2 ounces) grated Asiago cheese

1. Dissolve sugar and yeast in warm water in a large bowl; let stand 5 minutes. Lightly spoon flours into dry measuring cups; level with a knife. Add flours, milk, and next 3 ingredients to yeast mixture; beat with a mixer at medium speed until smooth.

2. Turn dough out onto a lightly floured surface. Knead until smooth and elastic (about 10 minutes).

3. Place dough in a large bowl coated with cooking spray, turning to coat top. Cover and let rise in a warm place (85°), free from drafts, 45 minutes or until doubled in size. (Gently press two fingers into dough. If indentation remains, dough has risen enough.)

4. Punch dough down. Cover and let rest 5 minutes. Turn dough out onto a lightly floured surface. Arrange olives over dough; knead gently 4 or 5 times or until olives are incorporated into dough. Cover and let rest 10 minutes.

5. Punch dough down. Divide dough into 16 equal portions. Working with one portion at a time (cover remaining dough to keep from drying), roll portion into a 2-inch ball. Place on baking sheets coated with cooking spray. Cover and let rise 30 minutes or until doubled in size. Uncover rolls, and cut a ¼-inch-deep "X" in top of each roll.

6. Preheat oven to 375°.

7. Combine 1 tablespoon water and egg white; brush over rolls. Bake at 375° for 18 minutes or until golden brown. Remove from oven; immediately sprinkle with cheese. Serve warm. Yield: 16 rolls (serving size: 1 roll).

CALORIES 161 (15% from fat); FAT 2.7g (sat 0.9g, mono 1.1g, poly 0.4g); PROTEIN 6.1g; CARB 27.5g; FIBER 1.3g; CHOL 4mg; IRON 1.6mg; SODIUM 212mg; CALC 58mg

A warm, fresh kalamata olive-infused roll sprinkled with rich, nutty-flavored Asiago is an ideal start to just about any meal. You can substitute Parmesan for Asiago and use green olives, if you prefer.

Pear, Pecorino, and Prosciutto Panini

1 firm, ripe pear, peeled, cored, and cut into 8 wedges
½ teaspoon sugar
1 (12-ounce) loaf focaccia, cut in half horizontally
4 teaspoons balsamic vinegar
1 cup trimmed arugula
½ cup (2 ounces) fresh pecorino Romano cheese, shaved
16 very thin slices prosciutto (about 4 ounces)

1. Heat a nonstick skillet over medium-high heat. Add pear to pan, and sprinkle with sugar. Cook 2 minutes on each side or until golden.

2. Brush cut sides of bread with vinegar. Arrange pear wedges, arugula, cheese, and prosciutto evenly over bottom half of bread; cover with top half of bread.

3. Heat pan over medium heat. Add stuffed loaf to pan. Place a cast-iron or heavy skillet on top of stuffed loaf; press gently to flatten. Cook 4 minutes on each side or until bread is toasted (leave cast-iron skillet on stuffed loaf while it cooks). Cut into quarters. Yield: 4 servings (serving size: 1 sandwich quarter).

CALORIES 383 (29% from fat); FAT 12.3g (sat 5.3g, mono 2.7g, poly 1.7g); PROTEIN 18.7g; CARB 50.8g; FIBER 2.7g; CHOL 40mg; IRON 2.8mg; SODIUM 1,019mg; CALC 178mg

Grilled and pressed sandwiches are compact and filled with flavor. From Italy to America, these sandwiches—called panini—are becoming increasingly popular. But you don't need fancy ingredients or equipment to make them. Use a cast-iron skillet (which you likely already have) or any heavy skillet to weigh down a sandwich in a nonstick skillet or grill pan. Place the skillet on top of the stuffed sandwich loaf; press gently to flatten. Cook 4 minutes on each side or until the bread is toasted, leaving the skillet on the stuffed loaf while it cooks.

Panini *(pah-NEE-nee)* technically translates as "rolls" or "little bread," but in Italy, the name is synonymous with sandwiches. The key to a good panino (singular) is high-quality bread, usually ciabatta, or in this case focaccia. Thinly sliced, rust-colored prosciutto, crisp garden green arugula, perfectly ripe pears, and freshly shaved tangy pecorino Romano cheese nestle inside crunchy focaccia. If you prefer cooked prosciutto, sauté it until it's crisp. Parmigiano-Reggiano makes a good substitute for pecorino Romano cheese.

Balsamic-Glazed Chicken and Bell Pepper Sandwiches

4 teaspoons olive oil, divided
½ teaspoon salt, divided
1¼ pounds chicken breast tenders
½ cup balsamic vinegar, divided
2 cups red bell pepper strips (about 2 medium)
2 cups vertically sliced onion (about 1 large)
2 (8-ounce) loaves focaccia, cut in half horizontally
4 ounces provolone cheese, thinly sliced
⅛ teaspoon black pepper

1. Heat 2 teaspoons oil in a large nonstick skillet over medium-high heat. Sprinkle ¼ teaspoon salt over chicken. Add chicken to pan; cook 1 minute on each side or until lightly browned. Add ¼ cup vinegar; cook 2 minutes or until chicken is done and vinegar is syrupy. Remove chicken mixture from pan; cover and keep warm. Wipe pan clean with a paper towel.

2. Return pan to medium-high heat; add remaining 2 teaspoons oil. Add bell pepper and onion; sauté 7 minutes or until tender. Stir in remaining ¼ teaspoon salt and remaining ¼ cup vinegar; cook 1 minute or until vinegar is syrupy.

3. Arrange chicken mixture evenly over bottom halves of bread; top with bell pepper mixture. Arrange cheese over pepper mixture, and sprinkle with black pepper. Top with top halves of bread. Place a cast-iron or heavy skillet on top of sandwiches; let stand 5 minutes. Cut each sandwich into 6 wedges. Yield: 6 servings (serving size: 2 wedges).

CALORIES 433 (24% from fat); FAT 11.4g (sat 4.2g, mono 5.4g, poly 1g); PROTEIN 34g; CARB 49g; FIBER 1.9g; CHOL 68mg; IRON 3.6mg; SODIUM 709mg; CALC 170mg

Sweet peppers, also called "bells," should have brightly colored, glossy skins. They should be free of soft spots and wrinkles, which are signs of aging, and their stems should be firm and green. Wash peppers just before you use them. Some bell peppers are waxed; scrub them well before eating. To cut a pepper into short, thin strips, quarter the pepper lengthwise and remove membrane, stem, and seeds. Cut each quarter crosswise into thin strips.

Balsamic vinegar cooks down to a glaze that clings to the sandwich fillings, adding a hint of sweetness and a touch of acidity. Pressing the assembled sandwich traps the heat from the cooked chicken and vegetables, which melts the cheese.

Corn and Smoked Mozzarella Pizza

The fresher the corn, the better it tastes. That's because as soon as corn is picked, its sugar starts converting to starch, which lessens the natural sweetness. So, it's important to buy corn as soon as possible after it's picked. Look for ears with bright green, snug husks, golden brown silks, and plump, milky kernels. Fresh corn is best cooked and served the day it's purchased. However, if needed, you can refrigerate it for no more than one or two days. Remove the husks and silks just before cooking.

2 ears shucked corn
Cooking spray
2 tablespoons olive oil, divided
¼ teaspoon crushed red pepper
1 garlic clove, minced
1 package dry yeast (about 2¼ teaspoons)
¾ cup warm water (100° to 110°), divided
2¼ cups all-purpose flour, divided
2 tablespoons 1% low-fat milk
1¼ teaspoons salt, divided
2 tablespoons cornmeal, divided
1 cup (4 ounces) shredded smoked mozzarella
1 cup very thinly sliced red onion
2 tablespoons chopped chives
1½ teaspoons grated lime rind

1. Prepare grill or preheat broiler.
2. Place corn on grill rack or broiler pan coated with cooking spray; cook 10 minutes, turning occasionally. Cool. Cut kernels from corn to measure 1 cup; set aside.
3. Place 1 tablespoon oil and red pepper in a small bowl; microwave at HIGH 30 seconds. Stir in garlic; set aside.
4. Dissolve yeast in ¼ cup warm water in a large bowl; let stand 20 minutes. Lightly spoon flour into dry measuring cups; level with a knife. Add 1 tablespoon oil, ½ cup warm water, 2 cups flour, milk, and ¾ teaspoon salt to yeast mixture; stir until well blended.
5. Turn dough out onto a floured surface. Knead until smooth and elastic (about 10 minutes); add enough of remaining flour, 1 tablespoon at a time, to prevent dough from sticking to hands (dough will feel tacky).
6. Place dough in a large bowl coated with cooking spray; turn to coat top. Cover and let rise in a warm place (85°), free from drafts, 40 minutes or until doubled in size. (Gently press two fingers into dough. If indentation remains, dough has risen enough.) Punch dough down; cover and let rest 5 minutes.
7. Preheat oven to 500°.
8. Divide dough in half; roll each half into a 9-inch circle on a floured surface. Place each circle on a baking sheet coated with cooking spray and sprinkled with 1 tablespoon cornmeal. Crimp edges with fingers to form a rim.
9. Brush dough portions evenly with oil mixture, and sprinkle with cheese. Top evenly with corn and onion, and sprinkle with ½ teaspoon salt. Bake at 500° for 8 minutes or until golden. Sprinkle pizzas with chives and lime rind.
10. Cut each pizza into quarters. Yield: 4 servings (serving size: 2 quarters).

CALORIES 473 (27% from fat); FAT 14.4g (sat 5.2g, mono 5.3g, poly 1.2g); PROTEIN 15.5g; CARB 70.2g; FIBER 4.5g; CHOL 23mg; IRON 4.3mg; SODIUM 788mg; CALC 194mg

Eggplant, Tomato, and Cheese Tart

Tart pans are shallow baking dishes with straight or fluted sides that produce a "professional" looking pastry. The best tart pans have a removable bottom, which will allow you to slip off the outer ring of the pan without damaging the tart's crust. Tart pans can be round or rectangular, and range from 4 to 12 inches across and from ¾ to 2 inches deep. A tart ring can be used in place of a tart pan. Tart rings only provide support to the edge of the pastry, allowing the bottom of the pastry to sit directly on the baking sheet while cooking. Tart rings are especially good for savory tarts, as they produce a much crisper crust.

Crust:
- 1 cup all-purpose flour
- 1 tablespoon toasted wheat germ
- 1 teaspoon baking powder
- ½ teaspoon freshly ground black pepper
- ¼ teaspoon salt
- ¼ cup water
- 1 tablespoon olive oil
Cooking spray

Filling:
- 1 (1-pound) eggplant, cut crosswise into ¼-inch-thick slices
- ¾ teaspoon salt, divided
- ½ teaspoon olive oil
- 4 garlic cloves, thinly sliced
- 1 tablespoon chopped fresh basil
- 1½ teaspoons chopped fresh oregano
- 1½ teaspoons chopped fresh mint
- 2 plum tomatoes, thinly sliced (about 6 ounces)
- ½ cup (2 ounces) shredded smoked mozzarella cheese, divided
- 2 tablespoons grated fresh Parmesan cheese

1. Preheat oven to 400°.

2. To prepare crust, lightly spoon flour into a dry measuring cup; level with a knife. Combine flour, wheat germ, and next 3 ingredients in a large bowl, stirring with a whisk; make a well in center of mixture. Add water and 1 tablespoon oil, stirring to form a soft dough. Turn dough out onto a lightly floured surface; knead lightly 4 times. Gently press into a 4-inch circle on plastic wrap; cover and chill 15 minutes.

3. Slightly overlap 2 sheets of plastic wrap on a slightly damp surface. Unwrap dough, and place chilled dough on plastic wrap. Cover with 2 additional sheets of overlapping plastic wrap. Roll dough, still covered, into an 11-inch circle. Remove top sheets of plastic wrap. Fit dough, plastic-wrap side up, into a 10-inch round removable-bottom tart pan coated with cooking spray. Remove remaining plastic wrap. Press dough against bottom and sides of pan. Pierce bottom and sides of dough with a fork; bake at 400° for 10 minutes. Cool completely on a wire rack.

4. To prepare filling, arrange eggplant on several layers of heavy-duty paper towels. Sprinkle with ½ teaspoon salt; let stand 15 minutes. Pat dry with paper towels; brush with oil. Arrange in a single layer on a baking sheet coated with cooking spray. Bake at 400° for 20 minutes. Stack on a plate; cover with plastic wrap. Let stand 7 minutes to steam.

5. Heat a large nonstick skillet coated with cooking spray over medium heat. Add garlic; sauté 1 minute. Remove from heat; stir in ¼ teaspoon salt, basil, oregano, mint, and tomatoes.

6. Sprinkle 2 tablespoons mozzarella evenly in crust. Layer eggplant and tomato mixture in crust; sprinkle with remaining mozzarella and Parmesan. Bake at 400° for 10 minutes or until cheese melts. Cut into 8 wedges. Yield: 4 servings (serving size: 2 wedges).

CALORIES 260 (30% from fat); FAT 8.8g (sat 3.1g, mono 4.2g, poly 0.9g); PROTEIN 9.8g; CARB 37g; FIBER 4.6g; CHOL 13mg; IRON 2.6mg; SODIUM 681mg; CALC 210mg

desserts

Macedonia di Frutta

Originally from the north-eastern Italian city of Bassano del Grappa, grappa is a brandy distilled from grape skins and seeds left-over from the winemaking process. Like wine, its flavor depends on the quality and type of grape used. Some grappa is aged in wood barrels, adding increased depth and flavor. It pairs wonderfully with the tastes and textures of fresh fruits, such as are in this Italian dessert.

2 cups (1-inch) cubed cantaloupe
1 cup (½-inch) pieces peeled peaches
1 cup sliced strawberries
1 cup blueberries
⅔ cup (½-inch) pieces peeled nectarines
½ cup fresh orange juice (about 1 orange)
¼ cup sugar
2 tablespoons grappa (Italian brandy) or brandy
1½ teaspoons grated lemon rind
2 peeled kiwifruit, quartered and sliced

1. Place all ingredients in a large bowl; toss gently to combine. Cover and chill 2 hours. Yield: 5 servings (serving size: 1 cup).

CALORIES 154 (4% from fat); FAT 0.7g (sat 0.1g, mono 0.1g, poly 0.3g); PROTEIN 1.8g; CARB 34.8g; FIBER 4.2g; CHOL 0mg; IRON 0.5mg; SODIUM 10mg; CALC 27mg

A true Italian meal often ends with fruit, although occasionally Italians do like to indulge in other sweet treats. You can use any combination of fruits in this refreshing dessert. Macedonia di Frutta literally means "mixed marinated fruit." Substitute two additional tablespoons of orange juice for the grappa for a nonalcoholic version.

Warm Caramelized Pears with Clove Zabaglione

There are many ways to core pears and apples, depending on how the fruit is being used. In this recipe, Bosc pears are halved and then cored. Using a melon baller, teaspoon, or paring knife, scoop out the seeds and membrane. Just before serving, spoon the delicate zabaglione over the cooked pear half so that the sauce pools in the center and on the bottom of the bowl.

1 teaspoon sugar
¼ teaspoon ground cloves
¼ teaspoon allspice
¼ teaspoon ground cinnamon
⅛ teaspoon ground nutmeg
½ cup sweet Marsala
3 tablespoons honey
1 tablespoon butter
2 pieces lemon rind (about
    1 x 3-inches long)
4 large Bosc pears, halved and
    cored (about 2 pounds)
Cooking spray
6 tablespoons sweet Marsala
¼ cup sugar
2 tablespoons water
⅛ teaspoon salt
4 large egg yolks
1 teaspoon butter
Lemon zest (optional)
Ground nutmeg (optional)

1. Preheat oven to 350°.
2. Combine first 5 ingredients in a small bowl; set aside.
3. Combine ½ cup Marsala, honey, 1 tablespoon butter, rind, and 1 teaspoon spice mixture in a small saucepan. Heat over medium heat until butter is melted.
4. Place pear halves, cut sides up, in a 13 x 9–inch baking dish coated with cooking spray. Pour Marsala mixture over pears. Bake at 350° for 30 minutes or until pears are tender, basting occasionally. Remove from oven; keep warm.
5. Combine 6 tablespoons Marsala, ¼ cup sugar, water, salt, and egg yolks in a medium, heavy saucepan, stirring with a whisk. Cook over low heat, whisking constantly, until mixture is thick (about 5 minutes). Stir in remaining spice mixture and 1 teaspoon butter until blended. Place 1 pear half in each of 8 bowls. Spoon ¼ cup sauce over each pear half. Garnish with lemon zest and nutmeg, if desired. Serve immediately. Yield: 8 servings.

CALORIES 196 (19% from fat); FAT 4.2g (sat 1.8g, mono 1.8g, poly 0.5g); PROTEIN 1.8g; CARB 33.4g; FIBER 3.4g; CHOL 107mg; IRON 0.5mg; SODIUM 58mg; CALC 25mg

Zabaglione (zah-bahl-YOH-nay) is a Venetian dessert sauce that's known as sabayon in France. Made of egg yolks, sugar, and sweet Marsala, this thin, frothy, versatile sauce is worth mastering. Here, we serve it with warm pears, but you can also drizzle it over other fruit, cake, or ice cream. Zabaglione is best enjoyed warm.

Lemon-Buttermilk Panna Cotta with Blueberry Sauce

Despite its name, buttermilk doesn't have butter added. Today, most buttermilk isn't churned from heavy cream. Instead it's "cultured," meaning it's created by fermenting pasteurized fat-free or low-fat milk with a friendly bacteria culture in the same way that yogurt and sour cream are made. Although buttermilk has a refrigerator shelf life of up to three weeks, it tends to separate, so shake it before you use it. To make a quick stand-in for buttermilk, stir 1 tablespoon of fresh lemon juice or white vinegar into 1 cup of milk, and let it stand for about 10 minutes or until the milk thickens and begins to curdle.

Panna Cotta:
Cooking spray
1½ tablespoons unflavored gelatin
1 cup whole milk
½ cup plus 2 tablespoons sugar
3 cups low-fat buttermilk
1 teaspoon grated lemon rind

Sauce:
½ cup apple juice
¼ cup sugar
1 tablespoon fresh lemon juice
2 cups blueberries
Mint sprigs (optional)

1. To prepare panna cotta, lightly coat 8 (6-ounce) custard cups with cooking spray. Sprinkle gelatin over whole milk in a small saucepan; let stand 10 minutes. Cook milk mixture over medium-low heat 10 minutes or until gelatin dissolves, stirring constantly with a whisk. Increase heat to medium; add ½ cup plus 2 tablespoons sugar, stirring with a whisk until sugar dissolves. Remove from heat. Add buttermilk and rind, stirring well. Divide mixture evenly among prepared custard cups. Cover and chill at least 5 hours or overnight.

2. To prepare sauce, combine apple juice, ¼ cup sugar, and lemon juice in a small saucepan. Bring to a boil over medium-high heat; stir until sugar dissolves. Reduce heat to medium; stir in blueberries. Cook mixture 8 minutes or until blueberries are warm and begin to pop. Cool sauce to room temperature.

3. Place a dessert plate, upside down, on top of each custard cup; invert panna cotta onto plates. Serve with sauce. Garnish with mint sprigs, if desired. Yield: 8 servings (serving size: 1 panna cotta and about ¼ cup sauce).

CALORIES 173 (10% from fat); FAT 2g (sat 1.2g, mono 0.6g, poly 0.1g); PROTEIN 5.4g; CARB 34.8g; FIBER 1g; CHOL 8mg; IRON 0.2mg; SODIUM 117mg; CALC 148mg

Well-loved throughout Italy, panna cotta (PAHN-nah KOH-tah) or "cooked cream" is traditionally made from heavy cream. However, for a lower-fat version we've substituted low-fat buttermilk and whole milk. Buttermilk creates a silky, tangy custard that's matched with a sweet berry sauce in this impressive make-ahead dessert. To make it easier to remove the custards from the cups, we recommend lightly coating the custard cups with cooking spray before filling and running a knife around the edge of each prepared custard.

Raspberry-Champagne Granita

2 cups fresh raspberries
2 tablespoons fresh lime juice
1½ cups water
1 cup sugar
¾ cup Champagne
Lime rind (optional)

1. Place raspberries and lime juice in a blender; process until smooth.

2. Combine water, sugar, and Champagne in a medium saucepan; bring to a boil. Reduce heat; simmer 1 minute or until sugar melts. Remove from heat; stir in raspberry puree. Pour mixture into a large, shallow baking pan. Cover and freeze 8 hours.

3. Remove dish from freezer, and let stand 5 minutes. Scrape entire mixture with a fork until fluffy. Garnish with lime rind, if desired. Yield: 6 servings (serving size: 1 cup).

CALORIES 152 (1% from fat); FAT 0.2g (sat 0g, mono 0g, poly 0.1g); PROTEIN 0.5g; CARB 38.9g; FIBER 2.8g; CHOL 0mg; IRON 0.4mg; SODIUM 3mg; CALC 12mg

Granita (gran-nee-TAH) is an Italian frozen ice made from water, sugar, and a fruit or wine flavoring. Rather than being smooth or creamy like a sorbet or gelato, a granita has more of an icy, or grainy, texture. Traditionally, it's stirred frequently during freezing to create large ice crystals. We've streamlined the procedure for this particular recipe. Simply remove the baking pan from the freezer and let it stand five minutes. Then scrape the granita with a fork (or two) until fluffy.

This frozen dessert, similar to sorbet, is easy to prepare, doesn't require an ice cream maker, and is almost fat free. Much of the alcohol evaporates during cooking, but the flavor of Champagne remains.

Honey Gelato

½ cup honey
⅓ cup nonfat dry milk
1 (12-ounce) can evaporated fat-free milk
⅛ teaspoon salt
4 large egg yolks
1 cup 2% reduced-fat milk
Mint sprigs (optional)

1. Combine honey, nonfat dry milk, and evaporated milk in a medium, heavy saucepan. Heat mixture over medium heat until honey dissolves, stirring frequently (do not boil). Remove from heat.

2. Combine salt and egg yolks in a large bowl; stir with a whisk. Gradually add honey mixture to egg mixture, stirring constantly with a whisk. Place honey mixture in pan; cook over medium heat until mixture reaches 180° (about 3 minutes); stir constantly (do not boil). Remove from heat; stir in 2% milk. Cool completely.

3. Pour mixture into freezer can of an ice-cream freezer; freeze according to manufacturer's instructions. Spoon gelato into a freezer-safe container. Cover and freeze 2 hours or until firm. Garnish with mint sprigs, if desired. Yield: 8 servings (serving size: ½ cup).

CALORIES 153 (19% from fat); FAT 3.3g (sat 1.2g, mono 1.2g, poly 0.4g); PROTEIN 6.7g; CARB 25.4g; FIBER 0g; CHOL 111mg; IRON 0.5mg; SODIUM 121mg; CALC 208mg

A commonly used natural sweetener for ages, honey is available in a diverse range of flavors and strengths. When choosing honey, a good rule of thumb is the lighter the honey's color, the milder its flavor. All honey crystallizes after it's been stored for a long time. To dissolve the crystals, place the container in warm water. Or, place small portions of the honey in a microwave-safe container, and microwave on HIGH for 2 to 3 minutes, stirring every 30 seconds. To make measuring honey easier, lightly coat your measuring spoon or cup with cooking spray so the honey will slide out.

Honey is a good choice for gelato because its resistance to freezing ensures creaminess. We liked mild clover and lavender honeys in this recipe. Store the gelato in an airtight container in the freezer up to one week; it won't freeze solid but will maintain a soft texture. Purchased pirouline cookies are a delicate accompaniment to this rich dessert.

Zuppa Inglese

1 cup powdered sugar
6 large egg yolks
6 tablespoons all-purpose flour
3 cups 2% reduced-fat milk
2 teaspoons grated lemon rind
1 (10-ounce) loaf angel food cake, cut into ¼-inch-thick slices
¼ cup grenadine or raspberry syrup
2 tablespoons Drambuie or cognac
2 tablespoons cognac
1 tablespoon white rum
2 ounces semisweet chocolate, chopped
¼ cup sliced almonds, toasted

1. Place sugar and yolks in a large bowl, and beat with a mixer at high speed until pale yellow. Gradually add flour, beating until smooth.

2. Heat milk over medium-high heat in a medium, heavy saucepan to 180° or until tiny bubbles form around edge (do not boil). Gradually add hot milk to sugar mixture, stirring constantly with a whisk. Return milk mixture to pan. Cook mixture over medium heat until thick (about 8 minutes), stirring constantly. Remove from heat. Stir in grated lemon rind.

3. Spoon ¼ cup custard into bottom of a 2-quart soufflé dish or compote. Arrange one-third of cake slices in a single layer over custard. Combine grenadine, Drambuie, cognac, and rum. Brush grenadine mixture over cake slices until wet. Spread 1¼ cups custard over cake slices. Arrange one-third of cake slices in a single layer over custard. Brush grenadine mixture over cake slices until wet.

4. Melt chocolate in small glass bowl in microwave 1 minute or until melted. Combine 1¼ cups custard and chocolate, and spread over cake slices. Arrange remaining cake slices over custard. Brush with remaining grenadine mixture. Spread remaining custard over cake slices. Sprinkle with almonds. Cover and chill at least 4 hours. Yield: 9 servings (serving size: ⅔ cup).

CALORIES 306 (26% from fat); FAT 8.8g (sat 3.5g, mono 3.4g, poly 1g); PROTEIN 7.9g; CARB 45.1g; FIBER 1g; CHOL 152mg; IRON 1.2mg; SODIUM 283mg; CALC 170mg

Grenadine is a sweet, thick, red syrup often made from pomegranates, but it's also sometimes made with other fruit-juice concentrates. Grenadine is typically used to add color and flavor to cocktails and nonalcoholic drinks such as Shirley Temples. Most brands are alcohol free, but check the label carefully if this is a concern, as both alcoholic and nonalcoholic grenadine are available.

This dessert (pronounced ZOO-puh ihn-GLAY-zay) literally translates as "English soup." It's a classic Italian trifle made with custard and chocolate layered with liqueur-soaked cake. The combination of liqueurs can vary, but there should always be something red such as grenadine. For a nonalcoholic version, substitute nonalcoholic grenadine and about ⅓ cup fresh orange juice for the liqueurs.

Chocolate-Cherry Biscotti

After baking the biscotti rolls the first time, remove them from the oven and cool slightly. Place the rolls on a cutting board and cut each roll diagonally into 20 (½-inch) slices, using a serrated knife or electric knife.

2 cups all-purpose flour
1 cup whole wheat flour
¼ teaspoon salt
1 cup sugar
3 large eggs
2 tablespoons canola oil
2 teaspoons vanilla extract
1½ teaspoons almond extract
⅔ cup dried tart cherries
½ cup semisweet chocolate chips
Cooking spray

1. Preheat oven to 350°.
2. Lightly spoon flours into dry measuring cups, and level with a knife. Combine flours and salt in a bowl, and stir well with a whisk.
3. Beat sugar and eggs with a mixer at high speed until thick and pale (about 4 minutes). Add oil and extracts, beating until well blended. Add flour mixture, beating at low speed just until blended. Stir in dried cherries and chocolate chips.
4. Divide dough in half; turn out onto a baking sheet coated with cooking spray. Shape each portion into a 10-inch-long roll, and flatten to 1-inch thickness. Bake at 350° for 25 minutes or until lightly browned. Remove rolls from pan; cool 10 minutes on a wire rack. Reduce oven temperature to 325°.
5. Cut each roll diagonally into 20 (½-inch) slices. Place slices, cut sides down, on pan. Bake at 325° for 10 minutes. Turn cookies over; bake an additional 10 minutes (cookies will be slightly soft in center but will harden as they cool). Remove from pan; cool completely on wire rack. Yield: 40 biscotti (serving size: 1 biscotto).

CALORIES 81 (22% from fat); FAT 2g (sat 0.7g, mono 0.6g, poly 0.5g); PROTEIN 1.6g; CARB 14.6g; FIBER 0.6g; CHOL 17mg; IRON 0.5mg; SODIUM 20mg; CALC 6mg

Biscotti, twice-baked Italian cookies, are delightful dunked in a cup of hot coffee. If you're a fan of dried cranberries, they make a great substitute for dried cherries.

Chocolate-Walnut Cake

Walnuts are the fruit of the walnut tree, which grows throughout Asia, Europe, and North America. There are two popular types found in North America: the English walnut and the black walnut. The English walnut is large, round, light brown, and has a shell that cracks easily. It's the more common variety and is sold in the shell or shelled, in halves or whole. To toast walnuts, place them on a baking sheet, and bake at 350° for 6 to 8 minutes until lightly browned and fragrant.

Cake:

Cooking spray
- ½ cup chopped pitted dates
- ½ cup unsweetened cocoa
- ½ cup boiling water
- 1 teaspoon instant coffee granules
- 1 (1-ounce) slice firm white bread
- ½ cup walnut halves, toasted and divided
- ⅓ cup all-purpose flour
- ¼ teaspoon salt
- ⅔ cup granulated sugar, divided
- 2 tablespoons canola oil
- 1 teaspoon vanilla extract
- 1 large egg
- 3 large egg whites

Glaze:
- ⅓ cup unsweetened cocoa
- ¼ cup semisweet chocolate chips
- ¼ cup boiling water
- 1 tablespoon dark corn syrup
- 1 teaspoon instant coffee granules
- ½ teaspoon vanilla extract
- 1 cup powdered sugar

1. Preheat oven to 350°.

2. Coat a 9-inch round cake pan with cooking spray, and line bottom of pan with wax paper. Coat wax paper with cooking spray.

3. To prepare cake, combine dates, ½ cup cocoa, ½ cup boiling water, and 1 teaspoon coffee granules; let stand 20 minutes. Place bread in a food processor; pulse 10 times or until coarse crumbs form to measure ½ cup. Place crumbs in a large bowl. Reserve 10 walnut halves for garnish. Place remaining walnuts in a food processor. Lightly spoon flour into a dry measuring cup; level with a knife. Add flour and salt to food processor; process until walnuts are finely ground. Add to breadcrumbs. Place date mixture, ⅓ cup granulated sugar, oil, 1 teaspoon vanilla, and 1 egg in food processor; process until smooth, scraping sides of bowl once. Add date mixture to breadcrumb mixture, stirring mixture well.

4. Beat egg whites with a mixer at high speed until soft peaks form. Gradually add ⅓ cup granulated sugar, 1 tablespoon at a time, beating until stiff peaks form. Gently stir one-fourth of egg white mixture into batter; gently fold in remaining egg white mixture. Spread batter into prepared pan. Bake at 350° for 25 minutes or until cake springs back when lightly touched. Cool in pan 10 minutes on a wire rack, and remove from pan. Remove wax paper. Cool completely on wire rack.

5. To prepare glaze, combine ⅓ cup cocoa and next 4 ingredients, stirring until smooth. Stir in ½ teaspoon vanilla. Cover and chill 1 hour. Gradually add powdered sugar to cocoa mixture, beating with a mixer at medium speed until smooth and thick.

6. Place cake layer on a plate. Spread glaze evenly over top and sides of cake. Arrange reserved walnut halves on top. Yield: 10 servings (serving size: 1 wedge).

CALORIES 280 (30% from fat); FAT 9.2g (sat 2.2g, mono 3.4g, poly 3g); PROTEIN 6.1g; CARB 45.5g; FIBER 1.2g; CHOL 22mg; IRON 2mg; SODIUM 103mg; CALC 26mg

all about
Italian

In this Cooking Class, we visit Italy, where tomatoes and olives rule, Parmigiano-Reggiano is king, and wine is a must. Fresh ingredients and simple techniques are key to one of the world's most loved cuisines.

It's true that Italians have a passion for life, and one of life's great pleasures is good food. Look, for example, at Italy's renowned food markets—the fresh local fruits, vegetables, and seafood make it clear that Italian food is all about using the freshest ingredients available and bringing out their flavors. It's a cuisine that runs the flavor gamut from rich and complex to light and simple.

Regional Cuisine

Italy is made up of 20 different regions, each with its own culinary flavors and traditions. And though the country is relatively small, the difference in the food from one region to the next is extraordinary. What you find in the north is different from central and south and vice versa.

Northern Italy

The cuisine in northern Italy tends to rely more on dairy products such as butter, cream, and cheeses because the land is flatter and better suited to raising cattle, sheep, and goats. Some of the creamy, rich cheeses include mascarpone and Gorgonzola from Lombardy, fontina from Valle d'Aosta, and Taleggio from Veneto. The region of Emilia-Romagna is known for its Parmigiano-Reggiano, considered by many to be the finest Italian cheese, and homemade egg pasta. It's also the region famous for prosciutto di Parma, as well as countless other cured meats and exquisite sausages.

Northern Italy is also one of the most affluent parts of the country, which may explain why some foods feature more expensive ingredients.

Central Italy

In central Italy, the food becomes heartier, with the wonderful bean soups of Tuscany and the savory roasted meats of Umbria and Abruzzo, where lamb, wild boar, and game are more prevalent than other meats.

Southern Italy

Cooks in southern Italy rely more on olive oil than butter and cheeses made from sheep's milk. Further south, the population is less affluent, hence you'll find fewer speciality ingredients, a more sparing use of meat, and a greater reliance on local, seasonal foods. Sicilian and Sardinian cooking aren't necessarily heavy, as is often thought. They're delicate, fragrant cuisines that emphasize the flavors of the fresh ingredients and seafood with which they're blessed.

The Italian Pantry & Garden

Italian cooking marries the joy of life with a love for simple foods. Fresh vegetables, fruits, and herbs combined with simple seasonings, good olive oil, and flavorful cheeses add gusto to the Italian table.

Olive oil is at the heart of Italian cooking, but it can be used for two very different purposes: as a fat for cooking and as a condiment for adding flavor to soups, sauces, vegetables, and bread. Cook with a less-expensive grade or "pure" oil. Always use extravirgin oil (the most intensely flavored from the olives' first pressing) when you want to *taste* it, for example, drizzled over a food just before serving.

Fresh **garlic** is a hallmark of Italian fare. Pick tightly closed, plump bulbs of creamy white garlic and store (away from other food) in a cool, dark place. Garlic will keep this way up to two months; however, once broken from the bulb, garlic cloves will last only a few days. Crushing garlic with the flat side of a knife releases its essential oils and provides the most assertive flavor for cooking.

Dried pasta is the quintessential pantry item: It boasts a long shelf life, is universally available, and offers variety from long strands of linguine and spaghetti to short tubes like penne to shapes such as orecchiette ("little ears"), cavatelli, and bow ties. When you have a choice between domestic and imported pasta, choose pasta imported from Italy. Premium brands of Italian-made pasta have a satisfying texture and the subtle flavor of semolina flour. When choosing egg pasta, avoid the "fresh" pasta sold in the refrigerated case in the supermarket. Either make your own or buy the dried noodles packaged in nests.

Arborio rice is the rice most often used to make risotto, but other varieties, such as Carnaroli or Vialone Nano, are perhaps even better. One characteristic they all share is a translucent, starchy exterior that melts away while cooking to give risotto its distinctive creamy consistency.

Canned **cannellini beans** (Tuscan white beans), jarred **marinara sauce**, an assortment of **vinegars** (including balsamic, red and white wine) and **capers** are all essential pantry items. A splash of sharp vinegar or a spoonful of capers adds that certain zing to finish many an Italian masterpiece for the table.

Fresh **plum tomatoes**, also called Roma or Italian tomatoes, have a lower water content and fewer seeds than other tomatoes. They're best for making homemade pasta sauce. If you must go for the pantry friendly version, stock up on 28-ounce cans of San Marzano tomatoes for authentic Italian flavor. San Marzano tomatoes are exceptionally juicy and aromatic—worlds apart from other canned tomatoes you'll taste.

Fennel, a licorice-flavored member of the parsley family, grows wild in many regions of Italy. The white bulb of the plant is one of Italy's most popular vegetables and it's especially delicious served raw in salads. (Cooking mellows the flavor.) Fennel seeds are a key seasoning for sausage and meatballs. They also lend a distinctive flavor to roasted meat and fish.

Fresh herbs are essential to Italian cooking. It's hard to imagine tomato sauce without basil, roast without rosemary, or beans without sage. Use fresh herbs as much as possible for the immediate punch of flavor they add to food. Storing fresh cut herbs is easy—trim about ¼ inch from the stem, and rinse with cold water. Loosely wrap herbs in a damp paper towel, then seal in a zip-top plastic bag filled with air and refrigerate. Check herbs daily, as some of them lose their flavor after a couple of days. The herbs should keep fresh for up to seven days. You may also consider placing herbs, stems down, in a glass with water (let the water cover about 1 inch of the stem ends); change the water every other day. Most herbs will keep for up to a week this way as well.

Dried herbs tend to have a more concentrated flavor. A good rule of thumb to remember is to use 1 teaspoon of dried herb for every tablespoon of fresh herb.

There are a handful of herbs that stand out from the rest as necessity in the Italian kitchen. **Italian flat-leaf parsley** makes a fresh addition to almost any savory dish, and it masks the odor of garlic. **Basil** is fundamental in tomato sauces, pesto, and many salads. It's in top form when married with tomatoes, as in the famous salad from the island of Capri—Insalata Caprese. It's one of the more perishable herbs, though its leaves are large and hearty. Once picked, it will only keep a few

oregano and thyme

days. **Oregano** is prized in southern Italy and widely used to season pizza, sauces, and vegetables. (If you opt for dried herbs, oregano is a fine choice.) **Thyme** is one to use sparingly to season meats, stuffing, marinades, and fish. Like rosemary, it has a prominent flavor. Simply strip the tiny leaves from the stem. **Rosemary** is popular in modern Italian cooking as a seasoning for roasts (lamb in particular), potatoes, breads like focaccia, and vegetables.

rosemary

Sage is abundant in Tuscan cuisine and is often used in tandem with rosemary to flavor meats and some bean dishes. Both sage and rosemary store easily up to a week in the refrigerator.

sage

Parmigiano-Reggiano

According to strict guidelines, only cheese that is produced in a limited area surrounding Parma may be sold as Parmigiano-Reggiano. Its incomparable flavor, texture, and richness make it an excellent grating cheese.

Essential Techniques for Making Pizza Dough

Homemade pizza dough (recipe on facing page) can be used to create the crust for your favorite pizza, to wrap a calzone, or to shape into a loaf of bread or focaccia (see Herbed Focaccia on page 26). Make the dough, and let it rise for an hour; or make it in the morning, and place it in the refrigerator until ready to shape and bake.

1. Gradually add about 2 cups flour to the yeast-flour mixture, stirring with a wooden spoon. You may need to add more or use less flour. A slightly sticky dough, though messy to handle, will make a more tender crust or bread.

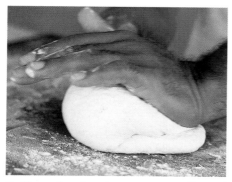

2. Turn the dough out onto a floured surface, and knead until smooth and elastic. To knead, push out the mound of dough with the heels of your hands, fold it over, give it a quarter-turn, and

repeat. Massage the dough gently. The dough should become smooth. If necessary, add slightly more flour while kneading. If you overwork the dough, it will absorb too much flour, producing a dense, heavy bread or a dry, tough crust. Set your kitchen timer for 10 minutes so you won't over- or underknead.

3. Place the dough in a large bowl, and let it rise in a warm place about an hour or until doubled in size. If your kitchen is chilly, place the bowl in a cool oven with a cup of boiling water or on top of the refrigerator where it's warm. The dough is ready when you can press it with two fingers and the indentations remain. Just prior to shaping, punch down the dough, and let it rest 5 minutes. This important step gives the gluten time to relax, making the dough easier to roll and shape.

To shape pizza crust, pat the dough with floured hands, or roll it with a rolling pin, starting at the center of the dough and moving toward the edge. Pat or roll the dough into the desired size, and transfer to a pizza pan. If you don't have a pizza pan, simply use a large baking sheet.

To make focaccia, roll out the dough, let it rise, and then make indentations in the top of the dough with a wooden spoon or your fingers.

All-Purpose Pizza Dough

This basic recipe can easily be doubled. You can also make it in a food processor or stand-up mixer with the kneading attachment.

    1 package dry yeast (about 2¼
       teaspoons)
 1¼ cups warm water (100° to 110°)
 3¼ cups all-purpose flour, divided
    ½ teaspoon salt
Cooking spray

1. Dissolve yeast in warm water in a large bowl, and let stand 5 minutes. Lightly spoon flour into dry measuring cups, and level with a knife. Add 1 cup flour and salt to yeast mixture, and stir well. Add 2 cups flour, 1 cup at a time, stirring well after each addition. Turn dough out onto a floured surface. Knead until smooth and elastic (about 10 minutes), adding enough of remaining flour, 1 tablespoon at a time, to prevent dough from sticking to hands (dough will feel tacky).

2. Place dough in a large bowl coated with cooking spray, turning to coat top. Cover and let rise in a warm place (85°), free from drafts, 1 hour or until doubled in size. (Press two fingers into dough. If indentation remains, dough has risen enough.) Punch dough down; cover and let rest 5 minutes. Shape dough according to recipe directions. Yield: dough for 1 pizza.

CALORIES 1,505 (3% from fat); FAT 5g (sat 0.8g, mono 0.7g, poly 2.1g); PROTEIN 44.6g; CARB 312.7g; FIBER 12.9g; CHOL 0mg; IRON 20mg; SODIUM 1,184mg; CALC 66mg

Herbed Focaccia

To Freeze Pizza Dough

To freeze, let the dough rise once, punch it down, and shape it into a ball. Place it in a heavy-duty zip-top plastic bag coated with cooking spray; squeeze out all the air, and seal. Store in the freezer for up to 1 month. To thaw, place the dough in the refrigerator 12 hours or overnight. With scissors, cut away the plastic bag. Place the dough on a floured surface, and shape according to recipe directions. Alternatively, for crust, you can make the dough, roll it out, wrap it in foil, and freeze. To bake, remove the dough from the freezer; top and bake according to recipe instructions (no need to thaw).

Essential Techniques for Making Homemade Ricotta Cheese

Ricotta cheese is easy to make, and after tasting the creamy results you'll find it's worth the effort. Use it in Ricotta Ravioli with Browned Poppy Seed Butter and Asparagus (recipe on page 62) or in other Italian favorites such as lasagna or manicotti.

Tips for Homemade Ricotta
(recipe on facing page)

• Buy a candy thermometer that can clamp onto the lip of the pot, which will allow you to obtain an accurate temperature reading as you heat the milk.

• Before heating the milk mixture, set out everything you need: a candy thermometer; a slotted spoon; a large piece of cheesecloth; a large colander or sieve; and a large bowl.

• Resist the temptation to stir the milk mixture after it registers 170° on the thermometer, or the curds that have formed will break apart, giving the ricotta a grainy, thin texture.

• Do not push on the curds while the ricotta is draining over the bowl; let excess whey drip out, then tie the cheesecloth into a bundle, and hang it over the faucet for 15 minutes.

• If your kitchen sink has a gooseneck faucet, lay a long wooden spoon or dowel across one corner of the sink, and hang the bag on the handle.

• Let the ricotta cool to room temperature before refrigerating.

• Use fresh ricotta within four days of making it.

• If you plan to make several batches of ricotta, always clean the pot between uses, and use a fresh piece of cheesecloth for every batch.

1. Immerse the tip of the thermometer 2 inches into liquid to ensure an accurate reading once the curds rise to the top.

2. Line a large colander or sieve with 5 layers of dampened cheesecloth, allowing the cheesecloth to extend over the outside edges of colander; place the colander in a large bowl.

3. Gather the edges of the cheesecloth, and tie into a bag; be careful not to squeeze the bag or push on the curds.

4. Hang the cheesecloth bag over the sink faucet to allow the whey to drain completely.

Homemade Ricotta Cheese
1 gallon 2% reduced-fat milk
5 cups low-fat buttermilk
½ teaspoon fine sea salt

1. Line a large colander or sieve with 5 layers of dampened cheesecloth; place colander in a large bowl. Set aside.
2. Combine milk and buttermilk in a large, heavy stockpot. Attach a candy thermometer to edge of pan so that thermometer extends at least 2 inches into milk mixture. Cook over medium-high heat until thermometer registers 170° (about 20 minutes), gently stirring occasionally. As soon as milk mixture reaches 170°, stop stirring (whey and curds will begin separating). Continue to cook, without stirring, until thermometer registers 190°. Immediately remove pan from heat. (Bottom of pan may be slightly scorched.)
3. Using a slotted spoon, gently spoon curds into prepared cheesecloth-lined colander; discard whey, or reserve it for another use. Drain over bowl 5 minutes. Gather edges of cheesecloth together; tie securely. Hang cheesecloth bundle from kitchen faucet; drain 15 minutes or until whey stops dripping. Scrape ricotta into a bowl. Sprinkle with salt; toss gently with a fork to combine. Cool to room temperature. Yield: about 3 cups (serving size: ¼ cup).
Note: Store in refrigerator up to 4 days.

CALORIES 115 (48% from fat); FAT 6.1g (sat 3.8g, mono 1.8g, poly 0.2g); PROTEIN 11.5g; CARB 3.5g; FIBER 0g; CHOL 23mg; IRON 0mg; SODIUM 191mg; CALC 250mg

Ricotta Ravioli

Commercial Ricotta
You can purchase both regular and part-skim ricotta in plastic tubs in the supermarket. These products are acceptable for recipes calling for ricotta cheese. Preservatives make this cheese less perishable. However, the richer taste and more compact texture of fresh ricotta sold in specialty food stores will come closer to what you can make at home. Buy fresh ricotta no more than a day or two before using it, and refrigerate immediately, as it's highly perishable. If it seems watery, drain by placing it in a cheesecloth-lined sieve set over a bowl for an hour or so in the refrigerator.

What Is Whey?
Whey is the light green liquid left behind when butterfat is separated from milk. When heating milk and buttermilk to make ricotta cheese, a thick, creamy layer (curds) forms on top, leaving the whey below. Whey is virtually fat free and contains some calcium, potassium, B vitamins, zinc, and magnesium. You can discard it or use it in place of water or milk in breads, pancakes, or muffins.

Sweet Ideas
Ricotta's creamy texture and mild flavor make it ideal for easy-to-prepare, healthful desserts and sweet snacks. Here are a few ideas:

• Serve ricotta atop pancakes or French toast, and drizzle with maple syrup.
• Spread ricotta on toasted slices of baguette or English muffin halves, and dust with cinnamon sugar.
• Whisk honey into ricotta, dollop in dessert goblets, and top with berries.
• Whip ricotta, unsweetened cocoa, and sugar until creamy; spoon into wineglasses, and garnish with toasted pine nuts and crumbled amaretti cookies.
• Combine ricotta, grated orange rind, and honey; spread on store-bought crepes, and roll up. Chill one hour or until firm, and cut into pinwheels.

Subject Index

Anchovy, 92
Antipasto, 36, 38, 42

Basil, 22, 137
Beans, 12
  cannellini, 12, 136
  fava, 18
  substituting canned for dried, 94
  white, 48
Beets, fresh, 74
Belgian endive, 52
Beverages. *See also* Grappa, Wine.
  alcoholic, 16, 24, 40, 90, 118,
    120, 128
  buttermilk, 122
Biscotti, 130
Breads
  ciabatta, 104
  focaccia, 26, 138
  yeast dough, 106, 138
Bruschetta, 10

Cacciatore, 100
Caesar salad, 54
Cantaloupe, 36
Caponata, 42
Carbonara, 64
Cheese, 135. *See also* Ricotta.
  mascarpone, 76, 135
  mozzarella, fresh, 14, 28, 72
  Parmigiano-Reggiano, 108, 135, 137
  smoked Gouda, 60
Chopping vegetables, 94
Clams, canned and fresh, 68
Corn, 112
Crostini, 44
Croutons, homemade, 54
Cuisine, Italian, 135

Eggplant, 16, 42
Eggs, cooking for carbonara, 64

Fagioli, 12
Fennel, 50, 136
Fish, red snapper, 84
Frittata, 30
Fruit, coring, 120

Garlic, 66, 136
Granita, 124
Grappa, 118
Grenadine, 128
Grilling
  grill pan, 82
  vegetables, 38
Gyoza skins, 62

Herbs, 137
Honey, 126

Ladyfingers, 32
Lasagna noodles, 70

Meat
  flattening and stuffing, 96
  thermometers, 90
Minestrone, 46
Mortar and pestle, 40
Mushrooms, porcini, 100

Oil and vinegar, 42
Olive oil, 56, 135, 136
Olives, 40

Pancetta, 30
Panini, 108
Panna cotta, 122
Panzanella, 56
Parsley, Italian (flat-leaf), 66, 137
Pasta, dried, 136
Pepper, bell, 110
  grilling, 38
Pesto, 22, 84
Pine nuts, 22
Pizza
  dough, 138-139
  freezing pizza dough, 139
  making pizza dough, 138
  Margherita, 28
Polenta, 20, 78
Prosciutto, 48, 135

Rice
  Arborio, 18, 72, 136
  risotto, 18, 72

Ricotta cheese, 62, 135, 140-141
  homemade, 62, 140-141
  making homemade ricotta cheese, 140
  salata, 62
  whey, 141

Sauces
  commercial pasta, 98
  dessert, 120
  puttanesca, 82
Scallops, 86
Shrimp, 88
Spaghettini, 66
Spices, crushing, 40
Substitutions
  basil for sage, 72
  canned beans for dried, 94
  canned lump crabmeat for
    fresh, 70
  cheese, 108
  dried cranberries for dried
    cherries, 130
  for alcohol in recipes, 118, 128
  for buttermilk, 122
  for mascarpone cheese, 76
  precooked lasagna noodles, 70
  shrimp for prawns, 88

Tart pans, 114
Testing for doneness, 84
Tiramisu, 32
Tomatoes, 10
  paste, 68
  plum (Roma), 28, 44, 84, 136
  rehydrating dried, 46
  slicing, 28

Veal, 24, 92

Walnuts, 52, 132
Wine, 16, 40
  in sauces, 90
  marsala, 24, 120
Wonton wrappers, 62

Zabaglione, 120
Zuppa Inglese, 128

Recipe Index

Appetizers
Antipasto, Grilled Vegetable, 38
Bruschetta, Tomato, 10
Caponata, Eggplant, 42
Crostini, Tomato, 44
Endive Stuffed with Goat Cheese and
    Walnuts, 52
Olives, Marinated, 40
Prosciutto and Melon, Minted, 36

Beans
Cannellini Beans, Lamb Shanks on, 94
Minestrone Bowl, 46
Panzanella, 56
Pasta e Fagioli, 12
Risotto, Spring, 18
White Bean Soup with Prosciutto,
    Tuscan, 48
Beef, Herb, Garlic, and Mustard-Crusted
    Fillet of, 90
Beet and Fennel Soup, 50
Beet Risotto with Greens, Goat Cheese, and
    Walnuts, 74
Blueberry Sauce, Lemon-Buttermilk Panna
    Cotta with, 122
Bolognese Sauce, Polenta with, 20

Breads
Panzanella, 56
Yeast
    Ciabatta, 104
    Focaccia, Herbed, 26
    Olive and Asiago Rolls, 106
    Pizza Dough, All-Purpose, 139
Butter and Asparagus, Ricotta Ravioli with
    Browned Poppy Seed, 62

Cacciatore, Chicken, 100
Carbonara, Spaghetti, 64
Casseroles
Lasagna, Seafood, 70
Ziti Baked with Spinach, Tomatoes, and
    Smoked Gouda, 60
Cheese
Chicken Parmesan, Herbed, 98
Endive Stuffed with Goat Cheese and
    Walnuts, 52
Insalata Caprese, 14

Panini, Pear, Pecorino, and Prosciutto, 108
Pesto, Classic, 22
Pizza, Corn and Smoked Mozzarella, 112
Pizza Margherita, Quick, 28
Polenta, Creamy Two-Cheese, 76
Polenta with Roasted Red Peppers and
    Fontina Cheese, 78
Ravioli with Browned Poppy Seed Butter and
    Asparagus, Ricotta, 62
Ricotta Cheese, Homemade, 141
Risotto with Fresh Mozzarella and
    Prosciutto, Sage, 72
Risotto with Greens, Goat Cheese, and
    Walnuts, Beet, 74
Smoked Cheese and Pancetta, Frittata
    with, 30
Spaghetti Alla Norma, 16
Tart, Eggplant, Tomato, and Cheese, 114
Chicken
Cacciatore, Chicken, 100
Glazed Chicken and Bell Pepper
    Sandwiches, Balsamic-, 110
Parmesan, Herbed Chicken, 98
Chocolate-Cherry Biscotti, 130
Chocolate-Walnut Cake, 132
Ciabatta, 104
Clam Sauce, Linguine with Red, 68
Corn and Smoked Mozzarella Pizza, 112
Croutons, Crisp, 54

Desserts
Biscotti, Chocolate-Cherry, 130
Cake, Chocolate-Walnut, 132
Gelato, Honey, 126
Granita, Raspberry-Champagne, 124
Macedonia di Frutta, 118
Panna Cotta with Blueberry Sauce, Lemon-
    Buttermilk, 122
Pears with Clove Zabaglione, Warm
    Caramelized, 120
Tiramisu, Instant, 32
Zuppa Inglese, 128

Eggplant
Caponata, Eggplant, 42
Spaghetti Alla Norma, 16
Tart, Eggplant, Tomato, and Cheese, 114

Fennel Soup, Beet and, 50
Fish. See also Clam, Scallops, Seafood, Shrimp.
Grouper with Puttanesca Sauce, 82
Red Snapper with Sicilian Tomato Pesto,
    Broiled, 84
Focaccia, Herbed, 26
Frittata with Smoked Cheese and
    Pancetta, 30

Garlic
Antipasto, Grilled Vegetable, 38
Bruschetta, Tomato, 10
Lamb Shanks on Cannellini Beans, 94
Minestrone Bowl, 46
Osso Buco with Gremolata, 92
Spaghettini with Oil and Garlic, 66
Gelato, Honey, 126
Granita, Raspberry-Champagne, 124
Greens, Goat Cheese, and Walnuts, Beet
    Risotto with, 74
Gremolata, Osso Buco with, 92
Grilled
Bruschetta, Tomato, 10
Vegetable Antipasto, Grilled, 38

Lamb Shanks on Cannellini Beans, 94
Lasagna, Seafood, 70
Lemon-Buttermilk Panna Cotta with Blueberry
    Sauce, 122
Linguine with Red Clam Sauce, 68

Melon, Minted Prosciutto and, 36
Microwave
Chicken Parmesan, Herbed, 98
Pizza, Corn and Smoked Mozzarella, 112
Minestrone Bowl, 46

Olives
Marinated Olives, 40
Rolls, Olive and Asiago, 106
Sauce, Grouper with Puttanesca, 82
Osso Buco with Gremolata, 92

Panini, Pear, Pecorino, and Prosciutto, 108
Panna Cotta with Blueberry Sauce, Lemon-
    Buttermilk, 122
Panzanella, 56

Pasta. *See also* **Lasagna, Linguine, Ravioli, Spaghetti.**
  e Fagioli, Pasta, 12
  Minestrone Bowl, 46
  Spaghettini with Oil and Garlic, 66
  Ziti Baked with Spinach, Tomatoes, and Smoked Gouda, 60
Pear, Pecorino, and Prosciutto Panini, 108
Pears with Clove Zabaglione, Warm Caramelized, 120
Peppers
  Bell Pepper Sandwiches, Balsamic-Glazed Chicken and, 110
  Roasted Red Peppers and Fontina Cheese, Polenta with, 78
Pesto, Broiled Red Snapper with Sicilian Tomato, 84
Pesto, Classic, 22
Pizza
  Corn and Smoked Mozzarella Pizza, 112
  Dough, All-Purpose Pizza, 139
  Margherita, Quick Pizza, 28
Polenta
  Bolognese Sauce, Polenta with, 20
  Cheese Polenta, Creamy Two-, 76
  Pork Saltimbocca with Polenta, 96
  Roasted Red Peppers and Fontina Cheese, Polenta with, 78
Pork Saltimbocca with Polenta, 96
Prosciutto
  Minted Prosciutto and Melon, 36
  Panini, Pear, Pecorino, and Prosciutto, 108
  Risotto with Fresh Mozzarella and Prosciutto, Sage, 72
  Soup with Prosciutto, Tuscan White Bean, 48

Raspberry-Champagne Granita, 124
Ravioli with Browned Poppy Seed Butter and Asparagus, Ricotta, 62

Risotto
  Beet Risotto with Greens, Goat Cheese, and Walnuts, 74
  Sage Risotto with Fresh Mozzarella and Prosciutto, 72
  Spring Risotto, 18

Salads
  Caesar Salad with Crisp Croutons, 54
  Endive Stuffed with Goat Cheese and Walnuts, 52
  Insalata Caprese, 14
  Panzanella, 56
Saltimbocca with Polenta, Pork, 96
Sandwiches
  Chicken and Bell Pepper Sandwiches, Balsamic-Glazed, 110
  Pear, Pecorino, and Prosciutto Panini, 108
Sauces. *See also* **Pesto.**
  Blueberry Sauce, Lemon-Buttermilk Panna Cotta with, 122
  Bolognese Sauce, Polenta with, 20
  Clove Zabaglione, Warm Caramelized Pears with, 120
  Puttanesca Sauce, Grouper with, 82
  Red Clam Sauce, Linguine with, 68
Scallops with Parsley and Garlic, Sautéed, 86
Seafood. *See also* **Clam, Fish, Scallops, Shrimp.**
  Lasagna, Seafood, 70
Seasoning
  Gremolata, Osso Buco with, 92
  Shrimp Scampi, 88
Slow Cooker
  Osso Buco with Gremolata, 92
Soups
  Beet and Fennel Soup, 50
  Minestrone Bowl, 46
  Pasta e Fagioli, 12
  White Bean Soup with Prosciutto, Tuscan, 48

Spaghetti Alla Norma, 16
Spaghetti Carbonara, 64
Spinach, Tomatoes, and Smoked Gouda, Ziti Baked with, 60

Tart, Eggplant, Tomato, and Cheese, 114
Tomatoes
  Bruschetta, Tomato, 10
  Crostini, Tomato, 44
  Insalata Caprese, 14
  Panzanella, 56
  Pesto, Broiled Red Snapper with Sicilian Tomato, 84
  Pizza Margherita, Quick, 28
  Sauce, Grouper with Puttanesca, 82
  Spaghetti Alla Norma, 16
  Tart, Eggplant, Tomato, and Cheese, 114

Veal
  Marsala, Veal, 24
  Osso Buco with Gremolata, 92
Vegetables. *See also* **specific types.**
  Grilled Vegetable Antipasto, 38
  Minestrone Bowl, 46

Walnuts
  Cake, Chocolate-Walnut, 132
  Endive Stuffed with Goat Cheese and Walnuts, 52
  Risotto with Greens, Goat Cheese, and Walnuts, Beet, 74

Zabaglione, Warm Caramelized Pears with Clove, 120
Zuppa Inglese, 128